PATRICK BRANWELL BRONTE

PATRICK BRANWELL BRONTE

By

Alice Law, F.R.S.L., F.R. Hist.S.
(Author of "Songs of the Uplands", etc.)

ISBN: 978-93-5128-597-7

First Published in 1923
Indian Reprint in 2017

Published by

Kalpaz Publications
C-30, Satyawati Nagar,
Delhi – 110052
E-mail: kalpaz@hotmail.com
Website: kalpazpublications.com
Ph.: +91-9212142040

Cataloging in Publication Data—DK
Courtesy: D.K. Agencies (P) Ltd. <docinfo@dkagencies.com>

Law, Alice, 1886- **author.**
Patrick Branwell Bronte / by Alice Law (F.R.S.L., F.R. Hist.S.).
pages cm
Reprint.
ISBN 9789351285977

1. Bronte˜, Patrick Branwell, 1817-1848. 2. Authors, English—19th century—Biography. 3. Painters—Great Britain—Biography. I. Title.

PR4174.B2L39 2017 DDC 828.809 23

CONTENTS

ILLUSTRATIONS

INTRODUCTION

In common with many other dwellers on the borders of the West Riding of Yorkshire, within a radius of some twenty odd miles from Haworth, I was brought up in the Brontë atmosphere. I have paid many visits to the little grey parsonage on the sky-line of the gaunt uplands, and every pilgrimage has intensified my profound pity for the unhappy life and blighted ambitions of Patrick Branwell Brontë, a feeling even predominating over my admiration for the genius of his sisters.

This feeling might have remained pity, and nothing more, had it not been at length roused to something warmer by finding such a torrent of unmitigated abuse of Charlotte's despised brother in all the Brontë literature, both present and past, as made one suspect there must be some source of irritation against him not immediately manifest to the general public. Yet the more I pondered over his case, the more inexplicable it became to suppose that the youth whom Mrs. Gaskell—a writer so near to the heart of things through her friendship with Charlotte—had pronounced to be "perhaps, to begin with, the greatest genius in this rare family", could have passed through nearly thirty-one years of life without leaving some work of value behind him. "To begin with"—the phrase is curious. One realises the suggestion behind it—that Branwell, both as boy and youth, gave promise of achievements which he never performed, and that having wasted and neglected his powers, he finally lost them. This opened up the question in my mind—Can genius perish utterly in a man? Even though the vessel be wrecked, will not some spars, some precious cargo float to land to shew what a rich-laden and goodly ship has foundered? What became of Branwell's undoubted genius?

In this perplexed state of mind I came across Mr. Francis A. Leyland's book on "The Brontë Family", written with especial reference to Branwell, giving various fragments of Branwell's work, and, most important of all, quoting his declaration that he had written a great portion of "Wuthering Heights."

The "murder" was out, and my suspicions concerning the marked animus shewn by the biographers of the Brontës—those of Emily in particular—towards Branwell, were at once confirmed. I began to understand something of the rage and indignation such an assertion would rouse in the minds of the staunch supporters of Emily's authorship, an authorship so confidently vouched for by Charlotte. I began to realize how necessary it was for the enthusiastic partizans of Emily and Charlotte to counter what Mr. Clement Shorter terms this "preposterous statement" of Branwell's, by endeavouring to shew him up as a thoroughly unreliable wastrel and liar. Greatly impressed with Mr. Leyland's very fair and balanced account of Branwell, I determined to study the matter more closely, with the result that I am convinced there is much evidence to substantiate his claim. To dismiss it as the biographers of Emily have done, with mere derision and rancorous contempt, is futile; abuse is not argument. It remains, therefore, in the interests of literary justice that Branwell's claim should be carefully examined, as I have endeavoured, how ever inadequately, to examine it in the following pages, and I venture to submit the accumulated evidence which has been brought to light since Mr. Leyland's day to the unbiassed judgment of my readers.

Where no absolutely direct proof can be adduced, I have employed conjecture; but only such conjecture as, taken together with all the obvious points of the case, amounts well nigh to certainty.

ALICE LAW

I

THE BIOGRAPHERS

THE history of the Brontë family, with one exception, that of their brother, the subject of this memoir, has been so often told as to call for little further comment. The story of Patrick Branwell Brontë, on the other hand, has but cropped up incidentally in the biographies of his famous sisters, hurriedly, apologetically thrust in, to illustrate certain aspects of, or crises in, their lives. The reference has been usually brief and damnatory, the pitiable narrative being introduced chiefly as a foil to display how their genius triumphed despite the stumbling block of a brother's disgrace, strewn in the path of their achievement.

Mrs. Gaskell passes him by with a shudder, referring to him as one who proved the bane of his sisters' lives; Sir Wemyss Reid, in his monograph upon Charlotte, refers to him as "this lost and degraded man"; Miss Mary Robinson (Madame Duclaux), in her study of Emily, cannot find words sufficiently scathing to convey her contempt for Branwell; and Mr. Swinburne, in his review of Miss Robinson's work, adds his invective to hers. Within the last quarter of a century other writers have gone out of their way to heap contempt and obloquy upon this unfortunate young man. Mr. Clement Shorter dismisses his pretensions to genius in the harshest fashion, and Miss Sinclair, relying perhaps too much on Mr. Shorter's judgment, and for a reason which I hope presently to make plain, acquiesces in, and even emphasizes the general condemnation. While at first generously deploring the perpetual digging up of poor Branwell, Miss Sinclair finally, in her study of "The Three Brontës", begins to dig as fast as any one, and to drive as many nails as possible into the coffin of his reputation.

Indeed, this necessity of repudiating Branwell has become a kind of obsession among Brontë writers, so much so that they seem to fear that unless Branwell is defamed, the sisters cannot come into their full inheritance of glory.

From what we know of Charlotte, Emily and

Anne Brontë, we can guess that they would owe their biographers scant thanks for such a miserable tribute to their reputation. Assuredly the lustre of their renown is brilliant enough, and needs no such deplorable foil. Yet, so it has been: from the time of Mrs. Gaskell until now, Branwell Brontë's failure has been everywhere emphasized to magnify his sisters' success or to enhance the pathos of their sufferings, until it is scarcely an exaggeration to say that his poor life and reputation have been used, much as were the bodies of some of the Early Christians—tarred with obloquy and burned as a torch to throw a more lurid light on the struggles of his kinsfolk battling in life's arena. His own martyrdom, at the hands of Fate and Family, has passed unheeded.

There is perhaps in the whole history of English literature—usually so generous to the claims of genius however handicapped by temperament or hampered by circumstance—no parallel instance of any writer of equal ability being subjected to the indiscriminate abuse heaped on Branwell Brontë. It is indeed time that all this execration should cease. Shameful if continued against the most ordinary human being, it becomes an outrage against the memory of one who had so little good fortune in his short lifetime; who died in his thirty-first year, a victim to the hereditary disease which devastated in turn the members of his family; and who left behind him fragments of art and literature which indicate the highest promise of what he might have attained in a more favourable environment.

Mr. Brontë was the first strongly to resent Mrs. Gaskell's uncalled-for attacks upon both himself and his son, and since then there have happily been a few gallant defenders of Branwell Brontë, to whose impressions the more weight may be attached since they either knew him personally or were in close touch with those who did. The report they render, taken as a whole, is markedly in his favour. The writers denouncing him, on the other hand, are those who have merely judged him from rumour and hearsay. Their almost hysterical outbursts against him leave the reader with the suspicion that they had some particular grudge against him, and, as I hope presently to shew, they undoubtedly have. The peevishness of these writers, makes them all, with the notable exception of Mr. Clement Shorter, strive to give their readers an impression that Branwell's whole life was a trial and disgrace to his family; whereas we know that only during the last three years, when he was suffering abnormal strain of physical and mental anguish, did he become a source of acute anxiety and distress to his father and sisters. For at least twenty-seven years he was the object of pride and dear affection. How he came to be anything less shall be examined later.

Before entering upon a discussion of Branwell Brontë's claim to our remembrance, a brief summary of his life history is necessary. Much material, previously unknown, has been brought together by the unremitting industry of his chief biographer, Mr. Francis A. Leyland, upon which* I shall not hesitate to draw largely, and base my own conclusions.

* "The Brontë Family" (Hurst and Blackett) 1886. Henceforth referred to as Leyland.

II

BOYHOOD

To begin then, as the children say, at the very beginning, it is known to all Brontë students that Patrick Branwell Brontë was born at the Parsonage House, Haworth, near Keighley, in the West Riding of Yorkshire, in 1818, the fourth child of The Reverend Patrick Brontë and Maria, his wife. He was called Patrick after his father, and Branwell after his mother's family. His mother died when he was three years old, and he can scarcely have had any definite recollection of her. From his fourth year onward, till he was old enough to attend the local Grammar School, we must picture the little Branwell as a fair, bright-eyed boy, with chestnut hair, sharing the home life of his five motherless sisters, under the kindly, but strict tutelage of their aunt, Miss Branwell, who at the request of her bereaved brother-in-law, had come up from Cornwall to manage his young family, and to preside over the affairs of his household.

It has been wisely said that every student of the Brontës would do well to visit the high moorland village where they were bred, a tiny rustic hamlet perched on the top of wild, sweeping, ruthless uplands, amid the kind of scenery that either attracts or utterly repels the onlooker. We know that in the case of one, if not two, of the sisters, their native moors were so much a part of their own nature, that they could not be happy elsewhere. This was not necessarily their brother's case, though the wild spirit of the moors undoubtedly imbued his mind and heart from lifelong association. As a tiny boy, hand in hand with his elder sisters, Maria, Elizabeth and Charlotte, he walked day after day along the roads leading either to Colne or Keighley, and when he was old enough to ramble alone or with some friend of his own age, we may be sure he frequented every nook and cranny that held Nature's secrets, and became acquainted with every bird and plant to be found in the remotest recesses of that desolate region.

It might be supposed that the only boy among a group of girls would be the especial object of his father's care and solicitude. It is clear that Mr. Brontë did his best for his son within the very narrow limitations of his somewhat stern and self-centred nature. But his whole system of training proves beyond the possibility of doubt, that he was no lover of children. His ideas were rigid, the little ones were not to come into close contact with him, he was to be "saved" from them, not to be disturbed by noise or play. To make quite sure that his solitude should not be encroached upon, he took his meals apart, and further to ensure that his offspring should prove sufficiently "tame" and docile, we are told that he kept them on a diet of porridge and potatoes. They were never allowed meat. Now in the mild climate of Ireland, where Mr. Brontë had been bred, and where so large a proportion of the population are potato-fed, this diet is probably fairly sustaining, at least when supplemented, as it usually is, with bacon. But for a bleak, bitter country like the desolate, high moors of the West Riding, such fare is quite unsuitable. The delicate children of the Parsonage needed the best food and clothing available, to protect them from the cold of that exposed region. It seems therefore impossible to exonerate this hard, self-absorbed parent from the grave accusation of having subjected his precious charges to a regimen and system of training which their tender bodies were totally unfitted to bear, and of having thus—unwittingly, it may be granted—laid them open to the ravages of that constitutional disease which proved fatal to them all.

In the case of Branwell, the lack of nitrogenous food was especially disastrous, as a boy needs more bone and muscle building, and there can be little doubt that the Spartan diet upon which he was reared induced the fragility so eminently noticeable in his constitution, both as boy and man. It was probably this lack of stamina and natural vigour which led him in later years to resort to stimulants that might spur his flagging energies, and which rendered him unequal to the strain of combating the series of disappointments he eventually encountered, under which his spirit broke completely and finally.

From all accounts he was a gentle, affectionate boy, but abnormally excitable. He was his aunt's especial favourite, but never taken into close companionship by his father. The grim old man did his duty, as he conceived it, by his son in grounding him well in the rudiments of learning, and without doubt taught him conscientiously and well. But his grave and reserved nature made him incapable of winning the boy's ardent, impulsive heart, and it was probably a relief to all concerned when Branwell was old enough to attend the local Grammar School.

It is well known from Mrs. Gaskell's work* how the children spent the winter evenings before bedtime. Seated together round the kitchen fire, they invented tales and little dramas; all

* "Life of Charlotte Brontë," by Mrs. Gaskell (Dent). With Preface by Miss May Sinclair, 1908. Henceforth referred to as "Life."

the children contributed some idea or other to the plays; but there is reason to suppose that Branwell was the leading spirit in their plots and composition, Charlotte taking the more tedious task of copying them out and preserving them in her private library. The names of three are given by Charlotte as follows: "Our plays were established: 'Young Men', June, 1826; 'Our Fellows', July, 1827; 'Islanders', December, 1827. These are our three great plays that are not kept secret."*

The titles of these plays indicate more strongly than anything the prominent part played by Branwell in their composition, though from Mrs. Gaskell's account, one might suppose the whole juvenile library, of which Charlotte writes, to have been her own sole creation. Branwell is also known to have contributed his share to the "Young Men's Magazine" completed December, 1829, of which six numbers are included in the "Catalogue of my Books up to August, 1830". It is more than probable that in speaking of these as her

* "Life," pp. 54-55.

books Charlotte was claiming possession rather than authorship, for it is known that her brother and sister Emily were equal contributors with herself.

The existence of these little compositions establishes the fact that Branwell, no less than his sisters, was engaged in romantic literary composition from the age of nine onwards. It is said that he was an ardent student and omnivorous reader of all the books or magazines that came his way. He studied the classics both with his father and at the Grammar School, and was a fairly brilliant scholar. Some of the magazines of the day, Blackwood's certainly, he saw, and the local papers; we also hear of his close acquaintance with the works of the great writers of the day, Scott, Southey, Wordsworth, Byron, De Quincey, Coleridge, Cowper, Burns, Christopher North, and many more, as well as with the classics of the Augustan Age and the great Elizabethans. It is remarkable, too, that, spirited boy as he was, his favourite poets were Wordsworth and Cowper: he was particularly fond of quoting the latter's poem, " The Castaway". A description given by Charlotte of one of her characters, Victor Crimsworth, in his boyhood, is said by those who knew, to have borne a close resemblance to Branwell as they remembered him. " Victor," she makes William Crimsworth say, " is pale and spare, with large eyes. . . . His shape is symmetrical enough, but slight. . . . I never saw a child smile less than he does, nor one who knits such a formidable brow when sitting over a book that interests him or while listening to tales of adventure, peril or wonder. . . . He had susceptibility to pleasurable sensations almost too keen, for it amounts to enthusiasm. . . . When he could read, he became a glutton of books and is so still. His toys have been few, and he has never wanted more. . . . I discovered in the garden of his intellect a rich growth of wholesome principles—reason, justice, moral courage, promised, if not blighted, a fertile bearing. . . . She (his mother) sees, as I see, a something in Victor's temper—a kind of electrical ardour and power—which emits now and then ominous sparks. Hunsden calls it his spirit, and says it should not be curbed. I call it the leaven of the offending Adam, and consider that it should be, if not whipped out of him, at least soundly disciplined. Frances, his mother, gives this some, thing in her son's marked character no name, but when it appears . . . in the fierce revolt of feeling against disappointment, mischance, sudden sorrow or supposed injustice, she folds him to her breast, or takes him to walk with her in the wood. Then she reasons with him, and to reason Victor is ever accessible. Then she looks at him with eyes of love, and by love Victor can be infallibly subjugated."* This is but a fanciful picture for which Branwell may have stood as the original, but if this was the case, we are brought in touch with a disposition that was obviously highly strung and sensitive to the utmost degree. An intense capacity for enjoyment was most certainly one of his characteristics, for we read of the wild exuberance of his spirits when, in the company of a friend, the son of a neighbour, he visited Keighley Fair. On a later occasion, when

* Leyland, I., pp. 83 *et seq.*

he had been sent by his father to escort Charlotte to a friend's house a few miles away, we learn that his ecstacy knew no bounds at the beauties of Miss Nussey's delightful home. "He walked about in unrestrained boyish enjoyment, taking views in every direction of the turret-roofed house, the fine chestnut trees on the lawn . . . and a large rookery, which gave to the house a good background—all these he noted and commented upon with perfect enthusiasm. He told his sister he was leaving her in Paradise, and if she were not intensely happy she never would be!"*

At this time he was between fifteen and sixteen years old.

This was a critical period in the boy's life. Beyond his years of childish tuition, he seems to have had no further help from his father, who, it must be granted, was in no way fitted by nature or temperament to have the up-bringing of so brilliant, wayward and impulsive a youth as Branwell. Consequently, out of lesson hours, he was left almost entirely to his own devices. In

* Ib. p. 115.

so retired and rural a hamlet what was there for the boy to do save consort with the youth of the place or listen to the coarse, if racy, conversation of the sexton, John Brown, who, being constantly employed in the graveyard, only a stones-throw from the Parsonage door, was always at young Master Brontë's disposal. The Sexton's "off" hours were largely spent in the bar-parlour of the Village Inn, and thither Branwell often followed him, either to hear his stories or to discuss Pugilism, a sport which has frequently a strong attraction for delicate boys striving to show they are as good fighters as any other. The "Noble Art of Self Defence" was much patronized in the early part of the last century by the fashionable dandies of London, as well as by the leading country gentlemen. Branwell, an enthusiastic boxer, was a member of the village Boxing Club, where no doubt he met many rough companions whose society cannot have been either suitable or beneficial to his temperament at this impressionable period of his life. Still, it is difficult to see how, without being a prig, he could have avoided the companionship of the youths who were his father's parishioners and Sunday scholars.

But though the rough and tumble life he shared with some of his village companions was undoubtedly a prominent feature of his early youth, there were other ties and attractions that bound him more closely: the attachment he had to his sisters, his affection for his devoted Aunt Branwell, and his respect for his father's teaching and character. At the Parsonage he spent his time cultivating his mind with all the good literature within reach, in the study of music, to which he was passionately devoted, and in the serious pursuit of art.

Branwell had lessons in music from the teacher who instructed his sister Emily—the only really gifted musician of the three sisters—and he also played the organ. Whether he played for the Sunday services is not related, but we hear of him at a later date, in 1837, officiating as organist at meetings of the Masonic Lodge of the Three Graces, held at Haworth in that year. He was particularly devoted to sacred music, and an enthusiastic admirer of the compositions of Handel, Hadyn, Mozart and other great masters. It is told of him that when the works of these great musicians were at any time played by his friends, he would walk about the rooms in an ecstacy, his eyes raised to the ceiling, "accompanying the music with his voice in an impassioned manner, and beating time with his hand on the chairs as he passed to and fro."*

Painting was, however, thought to be his greatest gift, and in company with his sisters, particularly Charlotte, Branwell had drawing lessons from a visiting master, and quickly proceeded on his own initiative to attempt oil painting. His gift for obtaining a likeness of his subject was very noticeable; indeed, so marked was his facility with brush and pencil that the whole family were convinced that art would be his vocation, and for several years he was strongly encouraged by them to persist industriously in its pursuit.

From all the accounts we have of his various

* "Leyland," I., p. 119.

accomplishments at the close of his boyhood, it can scarcely be disputed that Branwell Brontë was exceptionally gifted. He was, moreover, a boy who pulsed with feeling, a boy, who, while he danced with the joy of young life, vibrated also with all the emotions of sorrow when it visited the little domestic circle to which he belonged. In many respects he was as sensitive as a woman, and where he gave his affections, he became and remained passionately attached. The pathetic death of his two elder sisters, Maria and Elizabeth, when he was a boy of eight, made a tragic impression on his mind, and perhaps laid the foundations of that deep strain of dark melancholy that pervades all his poetry, and which plunged him in gloom at various intervals all through his life. His poems "To Caroline" are supposed to have been the outcome of his musings on the untimely deaths of his sisters.

It is scarcely to be wondered at if Branwell, marshalled as he was from a very early age in all his goings and comings by women, should have developed a marked sense of sex differentiation. Shut up as he was in a bare, dreary, moorland Parsonage; ruled over by a precise, formal and elderly lady, and a harsh-mannered, rude-voiced old Yorkshire house-wife, the famous "Tabby"; with no other companions than his three, delicate, prim sisters, trained in the strictest code of Victorian propriety; his father a grave, awe-inspiring elderly clergyman, absorbed more closely in his own personality than in that of his son—with such an environment, is it to be marvelled that he passionately longed for the society of his fellows, and that, the moment lessons were over, he rushed to freedom with all the glee and impetuosity of a wild thing escaping from prison bars? One can imagine him scampering over the moors, shouting aloud in sheer delight of living, strangely similar to that boy of whom Wordsworth wrote:—

> There was a boy—ye knew him well, ye cliffs
> And islands of Winander! Many a time
> At evening, when the earliest stars began
> To move along the edges of the hills,
> Rising or setting, he would stand alone,
> Beneath the trees, or by the glimmering lake;

THE MOORLAND TRACK.
Leading to what is now called "The Brontë Waterfall."

And there, with fingers interwoven, both hands
Pressed closely palm to palm, and to his mouth
Uplifted, he, as through an instrument
Blew mimic hootings to the silent owls,
That they might answer him * * *

And when it chanced
That pauses of deep silence mocked his skill,
Then, sometimes in that silence, while he hung
Listening, a gentle shock of mild surprise
Has carried far into his heart the voice
Of mountain torrents ; or the visible scene
Would enter unawares into his mind
With all its solemn imagery, its rocks,
Its woods and that uncertain heaven received
Into the bosom of the steady lake.

III

"I DON'T KNOW WHAT TO DO."

THESE words uttered listlessly by Branwell when he was a boy of between seven and eight, as he and his sisters were seated round the kitchen fire one winter evening, and which brought from Charlotte the bright suggestion that they should play at choosing an Island,* were almost prophetically significant of Branwell's attitude towards the various dilemmas in which he found himself at subsequent periods of his life. At the age of seventeen it became incumbent on him to choose a career. It may be supposed that his father would have been well satisfied had his son shown an inclination to qualify as a clergyman. But Branwell had no such desire either then or afterwards. It is probable that, this being the case, Mr. Brontë did not take the same interest in his son's future which he would have done had

* "Life," p. 53.

Branwell staidly adopted his own profession. But Charlotte, who was in a sense the leading spirit at the Parsonage, was at this time much impressed with her brother's abilities, and looked to him to accomplish great things. His gift for drawing was, so far, the most outstanding of his performances, and seemed to hold out the greatest chances of success. He had either at this time or a few years later, probably in 1839, made a life-size painting of his three sisters, which Mrs. Gaskell saw before it had faded, and of which she writes as follows: "It was a group of his sisters, life-size, three-quarter length; not much better than sign-painting as to manipulation, but the likenesses were, I should think, admirable. I could only judge of the fidelity with which the other two were depicted from the striking resemblance which Charlotte . . . standing right behind it, bore to her own representation, though it must have been ten years or more since the portraits were taken. . . . They were good likenesses, however badly executed. From whence I should guess his family augured truly that, if Branwell had but the opportunity . . . he might turn out a great painter."*

After, we may be sure, a most careful consideration of the question, it was decided that Branwell should seek entry as a student at the Royal Academy Schools, and he accordingly wrote to the secretary for information. All we know further is that in 1835 he proceeded to London with a view to presenting himself as a student, and that within a week he returned to the Parsonage without having achieved the exciting purpose for which he had so high-heartedly set out. To those who know the qualifying conditions of study at the Academy Schools there will appear nothing singular in Branwell's sudden return, though his detractors, hastening to use even this for the purpose of defaming him, and, without a shadow of foundation for their assertions, insidiously suggest that his failure was the outcome of indulgence in a course of dissipation at the first opportunity that presented itself.

Mrs. Gaskell in this connection writes absolute

* "Life," p. 88.

nonsense about "sisters who have laid their lives as a sacrifice before their brother's idolised wish," which is nothing to the point, as his sisters were in no way affected by Branwell's application at the Academy Schools, though they might have been had he selfishly decided to remain there and go through the necessary course of training. But to talk of "sacrifice" is ridiculous: some opportunity of training for a profession was in any case due to the boy if he were to support himself in life, and had he decided to enter the Church, he would have needed some course of college training. But this week in London was all he got, and yet Miss Sinclair talks glibly about his having "had his chance".* Even Mr. Shorter makes the totally unsupported assertion that the youth "probably wasted the money and his father refused supplies."†

Mr. Leyland, however, writes with sense and judgment upon the matter, and he has an especial right to do so, as his brother, the sculptor, was then

* Sinclair, "The Three Brontës," p. 17 (Hutchinson).
† Shorter, "The Brontë Circle" (Dent).

living in London, in close touch with some of the greatest artists of the day; and it is more than probable that under his patronage the lad made this first venture. "It would," says Mr. Leyland, "seem scarcely possible that the difficulties attending Branwell's admission as a student at the Royal Academy had been duly considered. He could not be admitted without a preliminary examination of his drawings from the antique and the skeleton, to ascertain if his ability as a draughtsman was of such an order as would qualify him for studentship; and if successful in this, he would be required to undergo a regular course of education and to pass through the various schools where professors and academicians attended to give instruction. No doubt it was wished that Branwell should have a regular and prolonged preparation for his professional, artistic career; but it would have lasted for years and the pecuniary strain consequent upon it would perhaps have been severely felt, even if Branwell's genius had justified the outlay."*

* "Leyland," I., p. 142–146.

It is greatly to Branwell's credit that he at once grasped this aspect of the case. He probably talked the matter over with the sculptor—afterwards his life-long friend—and decided that he was not justified in putting such a strain upon his father's resources, and so, after a wonderful week of sight-seeing in the city of his dreams, he made the best of it, and bravely returned to Haworth. This was indeed the only manly course to take, and he took it. But the boy's own bitter disappointment and disillusion may be better imagined than expressed, and we know that he referred to it in a conversation with his friend, Mr. George Searle Phillips, who mentions it in his account of Branwell published in the "Mirror" for 1872.

Branwell was not immediately discouraged. He could not afford London, but an arrangement was made, possibly by the generosity of his aunt, Miss Branwell, by which he should take a short course of lessons in Bradford, in the studio of the artist who had previously given him and Charlotte some occasional lessons at Haworth. He worked with Mr. Robinson for a few months, and then, possibly fired by the example of the great Chantry's humble beginnings, he started as portrait painter on his own account in that town. Although he received certain commissions, and lived frugally, it was not possible to make a profitable business out of so precarious an occupation; the days of black-and-white work, in which he would probably have excelled, had not yet come; and after a heart-breaking struggle, Branwell, in 1839, decided to abandon the pursuit of art altogether.

Miss Sinclair dismisses Branwell's art career very jauntily. "He went to London," she says, "but nothing came of it. He went to Bradford and had a studio there, but nothing came of it."* Nothing for Branwell possibly, but, I venture to think, much for ourselves. Had it not been for Branwell's great gift, not of painting, perhaps, but of portraiture, how much poorer should we be to-day! For is it not to his gift of perception and insight which found in the countenances of his three sisters something arresting, something akin to greatness, perceived by no one else, that

* "The Three Brontës," p. 17.

EMILY BRONTË.

From a painting by Patrick Branwell Brontë.

(Reproduced by kind permission of the National Portrait Gallery, London.)

we have preserved for us, although in ruins, the group of the three Brontës which Mrs. Gaskell saw and described in its first freshness? This we owe assuredly to the Bradford period. And if Branwell had no other fame, he has at least one species of immortality as the painter of his sister Emily's profile portrait, in which he has caught the very soul and spirit of his subject, and given her to us in all her Dantesque severity and aloofness, given her to us clothed with all the fatality of a Greek tragic figure, a second Antigone, gazing intently into Eternity. Only an innately fine artist could have given us this; the colours have perished, but the flame-like spirit of Emily remains and fires the faded canvas. Who, having seen even the wreck of this portrait of Emily Brontë can be unmindful of the undeveloped genius of the artist brother who conceived and limned it? Who, having dwelt on the truth of its execution, and the inexhaustible wonder of its subject, can truthfully say that "nothing came" of Branwell Brontë's art studies at Bradford?

While at Bradford he made many friends among

the most cultured artistic circles to be found there. His musical abilities also won him many friends in the town. Those who knew him there describe him as "a quiet, unassuming young man, retiring and diffident, seeming rather of a passive nature and delicate constitution than otherwise." Miss Mary F. Robinson's statements that he left the town heavily in debt, and was both a drunkard and an opium-eater are, says Mr. Leyland "simply untrue." "I have," he goes on to say, "the positive information of one who knew Branwell in Leeds, and who resided in Bradford when he was there, that he did not leave that town in debt; that he certainly was not a drunkard, and that if he took anything at all it was but occasionally, and then no more than the commonest custom would permit." In conclusion, Mr. Leyland speaks with admiration of Branwell's "honest, upright and honourable endeavour to make a living by the profession of Art at Bradford."*

Other forces were at this time also working in Branwell's mind. He had, since boyhood, never

* "Leyland," I., p. 178.

ceased the writing of tales and romances. As late as this Bradford period, he had written a story entitled " Percy". He continually produced poems, most of them tinged with that constitutional melancholy which was one of his most abiding characteristics. Great powers were undoubtedly stirring within him, but he was, his Bradford friends noted, diffident ; the source of this want of self-confidence may very well have been the undoubted frailty of his constitution, already pre-disposed to a consumptive tendency. None the less, his spirit was brave, and he left no means untried to discover what career he might adopt which would enable him to relieve his father from the burden of supporting him.

It was during what we may call this " Bradford Period " that Branwell occupied his available leisure in literary—chiefly poetic—attempts. Being very anxious to succeed, and scarcely knowing to whom to turn for guidance, he wrote to Wordsworth, and, enclosing some of his verses, ventured to solicit his opinion as to whether he was justified in pursuing his literary ambitions. I give the letter in full, as I think it is valuable evidence of one side of Branwell's character, a side which has been so little brought into prominence by his many detractors:*

" HAWORTH, NEAR BRADFORD.
YORKSHIRE,
January 19th, 1837.

" SIR,

" I most earnestly entreat you to read and pass your judgment upon what I have sent you, because from the day of my birth to this, the nineteenth year of my life, I have lived among secluded hills, where I could neither know what I was or what I could do. I read for the same reason that I ate or drank—because it was a real craving of nature; I wrote on the same principle as I spoke, out of the impulse and feelings of the mind; nor could I help it, for what came, came out, and there was the end of it. For as to self-conceit, that could not receive food from flattery, since to this hour not half-a-dozen people in the world know that I have penned a line.

* Gaskell, " Life," p. 98-99.

"But a change has taken place now, Sir; and I am arrived at an age wherein I must do something for myself: the powers I possess must be exercised to a definite end, and as I don't know them myself, I must ask of others what they are worth. Yet there is not one here to tell me; and still, if they are worthless, time will henceforth be too precious to be wasted on them.

"Do pardon me, Sir, that I have ventured to come before one whose works I have most loved in our literature, and who most has been with me a divinity of the mind, laying before him one of my writings, and asking of him a judgment of its contents. I must come before someone from whose sentence there is no appeal; and such a one is he who has developed the theory of poetry as well as its practice, and both in such a way as to claim a place in the memory of a thousand years to come.

"My aim, Sir, is to push out into the open world, and for this I trust not poetry alone—that might launch the vessel, but could not bear her on; sensible and scientific prose, bold and vigorous efforts in my walk in life, would give a further title to the notice of the world; and then again, poetry ought to brighten and crown that name with glory; but nothing of all this can be ever begun without means, and as I don't possess these I must in every shape strive to gain them. Surely in this day, when there is not a *writing* poet worth a sixpence, the field must be open, if a better man can step forward.

"What I send you is the Prefatory Scene of a much longer subject, in which I have striven to develop strong passions and weak principles struggling with a high imagination and acute feelings, till, as youth hardens towards old age, evil deeds and short enjoyments end in mental misery and bodily ruin. Now, to send you the whole of this would be a mock upon your patience; what you see does not even pretend to be more than the description of an imaginative child. But read it, Sir; and, as you would hold a light to one in utter darkness, as you value your own kind-heartedness, return me an answer if but one word, telling me whether I should write on, or write no more. Forgive undue warmth, because my feelings in this matter cannot be cool; and believe me, Sir, with deep respect,

"Your really humble servant,

"P. B. BRONTË."

Mr. Shorter has referred very slightingly to Branwell's letters in comparison with his sister Charlotte's, but I think no one can read the one I have just quoted without being touched by its tone of courteous deference and the lucid beauty of its style. The paragraph in which he asks Wordsworth to pardon his appeal is one of remarkable grace, and there are many other passages in the letter, particularly towards the close, that are affecting by the natural, simple eloquence of their entreaty. A youth of nineteen who could write so well as this had assuredly a future before him, if he could but meet with sufficient opportunities of exercising his already uncommon gifts of literary expression.

But one of the outstanding disadvantages from which Branwell Brontë suffered throughout his life was that—as he confessed so naïvely in this letter—he did not know what powers he possessed, and when he was on the verge of discovering them, misfortunes assailed him, and he died without coming into the heritage actually awaiting him.

Soon after his return from Bradford, we find Branwell accepting the situation of tutor in the family of a Mr. Postlethwaite of Broughton-in-Furness, and entering upon his duties there on the first of January, 1840. While in this neighbourhood it is recorded that he tramped among the lovely hills and valleys of that beautiful country, and it is suggested that he may have been received by Wordsworth, for whom, as we have seen, he cherished a deeply reverent admiration. He certainly was acquainted with Hartley Coleridge, who gave him a favourable opinion upon some work he had submitted. His mind continued to be occupied chiefly with literature, and he wrote his poem on "Black Comb" at this time.

It was while he was at Broughton that Branwell sent his old friend and crony, John Brown, the letter which so scandalized Miss Mary F. Robinson. It was written in a roystering, devil-may-care spirit, probably to throw off, for an hour at least, the constraint of solemn behaviour, unnatural to any young man of his age, which, in his position as tutor, he was obliged to assume. It was never meant for publication, but being proudly treasured in the sexton's family, has been given to the world.

Mrs. Gaskell, writing of Branwell as he appeared to his family about the year 1840, says: "At this time the young man seemed to have his fate in his own hands. He was full of noble impulses, as well as of extraordinary gifts; not accustomed to resist temptation, it is true, from any higher motive than strong family affection, but showing so much power of attachment to all about him, that they took pleasure in believing that after a time he would 'right himself', and that they should have pride and delight in the use he would then make of his splendid talents; . . . in early youth his power of attracting and attaching people was so great that few came in contact with him who were not so much dazzled by him as to be desirous of gratifying whatever wishes he expressed. . . . I have seen Branwell's profile; it is what would be generally esteemed very handsome; the forehead is massive, the eye well set, and the expression of it fine and intellectual; the nose too is good; but there are coarse lines about the mouth, while the slightly retreating chin conveys an idea of weakness of will. His hair and complexion were sandy. He had enough Irish blood in him to make his manners frank and genial, with a kind of natural gallantry about them. In a fragment of one of his manuscripts which I have read, there is a justness and felicity of expression which is very striking. It is the beginning of a tale and the actors in it are drawn with much of the grace of characteristic portrait-painting in perfectly pure and simple language, which distinguishes so many of Addison's papers in the *Spectator*. . . . But altogether the elegance and composure of style are such as one would not have expected from this vehement and ill-fated young man. He had a stronger desire for literary fame burning in his heart than even that which occasionally flashed up in his sister's. He tried various outlets for his talents. . . . In 1840 he was living at home, employing himself in occasional composition of various kinds, and waiting till some employment for which he might be fitted without any expensive course of preliminary education, should turn up."*

There are, I think, a few points in Mrs. Gaskell's description which seem to invite attention. It will be seen how much she admired Branwell's prose style, but it will also be noticed that she was so afraid of bestowing unqualified praise upon one whom she regarded as a backslider, that she modifies it with the expression of her astonishment at finding it so good. What connection there can be between an author's personal ill-fortune and his method of writing is difficult to conjecture. What is made plain by Mrs. Gaskell is that Branwell possessed a captivating personality, and a fascination of manner which goes far to explain much that subsequently befell him.

* "Life," 123-4.

Another point that calls for notice is the obvious determination of Mr. Brontë not to spend any money on preparing his son for any of the professions. We hear that the old gentleman was never weary of relating how he had managed to make his way to Cambridge and win his degree. But possibly he omitted to tell of the kind patron he had in the vicar of his native parish, a certain Mr. Tighe, by the aid of whose interest and liberality he had been able to be admitted to the University. The obvious thing would have been to send Branwell to try his fortune at Cambridge, even for a year. With the help of his aunt it would have been possible to raise the money for a year's course at least, and such a brilliant youth as Branwell would assuredly have repaid the training. But the only available capital was Miss Branwell's savings, and that was shortly to be annexed by that vehement individualist, his sister Charlotte, when she persuaded her aunt to advance £100 or more, to enable her and Emily to study at Brussels. She even refers to her father's ambitions to enforce her argument. "I want us *all* to get on," she writes.

Such a sum spent in getting Branwell out of the wretched village influences into a scholarly environment, where he could have absorbed the culture for which he so ardently hungered, might have altered the whole course of his life. It was certainly not the sisters who were sacrificed. The boy was mis-handled from his earliest years. He had no suitable guide or counsellor in his father, who was too self-absorbed to concern himself with his boy's future, and who, having sown neglect, reaped the harvest he might have expected.

Mrs. Gaskell refers to Branwell as being at home in the year 1840. He was there only from June till October, having at his father's instance resigned his appointment at Broughton only six months after he had received it. Meanwhile, as Mrs. Gaskell tells us, he was occupying himself in "occasional composition". By a strange and most fortunate chance some of these "compositions" have come into the possession of a critic competent in the highest degree to pronounce upon them. Mr. John Drinkwater has discovered, edited and privately printed* a newly found MS. of Branwell Brontë's, signed by him, and dated "Haworth, Nr. Bradford, Yorks, June 27th, 1840." This MS. is nothing less than a verse translation of "The Odes of Quintus Horatius Flaccus," all but the last, of which Branwell says, to quote from Mr. Drinkwater's volume: "This Ode I have no heart to attempt, after having heard Mr. H. Coleridge's translation, on May Day, at Ambleside."

Mr. Drinkwater supposes that most of these translations were made while Branwell was at Mr. Postlethwaite's, and probably the remainder at Haworth, after he returned home, and he finds these verses to be Branwell's "best achievement, so far as we can judge, as a poet." They are, he says, unequal, "but they also have a great many passages of clear lyrical beauty, and they

* As only fifty copies have been issued, I have not been able to examine Branwell's Translations, but Mr. Drinkwater most courteously allowed me to see a copy of his Introduction, from which I have made the above extracts.

have something of the style that comes from a spiritual understanding, as apart from merely formal knowledge, of great models." After passing in brief review the various verse translations of Horace from Ben Jonson to John Conington, whom Mr. Drinkwater regards as the "most consistently attractive" of them all, he adds: "Branwell Brontë's Translations of the First Book of Odes need, at their best, fear comparison with none."

Of at least half the Odes, Mr. Drinkwater goes on to say: "They are excellent in themselves and as good as any English versions that I know, including Conington's. In a few instances, I should say that they are decidedly the best of all . . . in some whole poems, as in the lovely rendering of xxi, there is hardly a flaw from beginning to end. At his best he has melody and phrase, and he builds his stanzas well. . . . The book adds appreciably to the evidence that Branwell Brontë was the second poet in his family and a very good second at that, and it leaves no justification for anyone to say that he 'composed nothing which gives him the slightest claim to the most inconsiderable niche in the temple of literature.' "*

Branwell spent the summer of 1840 in anxious enquiry after a new kind of occupation, and finally obtained a post as Clerk-in-Charge at one of the tiny new stations on the Leeds and Manchester Railway. He commenced his duties at this place, Sowerby Bridge, on the first of October, with great zest, but perhaps without realising to the full how extremely unsuited he was both by training and temperament for the kind of responsibility he had undertaken. He was above all things, anxious for some remunerative work by which he might be able to support himself, as he now did for the next two years.

The strenuous efforts of Branwell to obtain employment—even employment highly distasteful to him—do him the highest credit. He did not lose an hour in seeking to find some outlet for his energy, and to earn an income which, if

* Quoted from Mr. Clement Shorter's account of Branwell Brontë, in " The Brontës and their Circle," p. 113.

it did not enable him to save, at least kept him from being a burden on his father.

But as regards the duties attached to the post, light as they were, they were strangely unsuitable and tiresome to a youth of his excitable and poetic temperament. His heart could not be in them as, in duty to his employers, it should have been. He was temptingly near Halifax, where his friend Leyland lived, and he often went over to see him, After a time he was moved to another charge, to the care of the new halting-place at Luddenden Foot, where he had to spend all day in a miserable wooden shanty, stuffy in summer, and penetrated by wind and rain in the spring, winter and autumn months, a residence extremely unfitted for a youth so constitutionally delicate as Branwell Brontë. While he was employed at Sowerby Bridge, Mr. Francis Leyland was taken by his brother, the sculptor, to see Branwell at the station there. He gives us his impressions of him as he appeared in the autumn of the year 1840.

"The young railway clerk was of gentleman-like appearance, and seemed to be qualified for a much better position than the one he had chosen. In stature he was a little below the middle height, not 'almost insignificantly small' as Mr. Grundy states. . . . He was slim and agile in figure yet of well-formed outline. His complexion was clear and ruddy, and the expression of his face, at the time, lightsome and cheerful. His voice had a ringing sweetness, and the utterance and use of his English was perfect. Branwell appeared to be in excellent spirits, and shewed none of those traces of intemperance with which some writers have unjustly credited him about this period of his life.

My brother had often spoken to me of Branwell's poetical abilities, his conversational powers and the polish of his education; and, on a personal acquaintance, I found nothing to question in this estimate of his mental gifts and of his literary attainments."*

Another personal impression of Branwell when he was at Luddenden Foot, is given by Mr. William Heaton, who knew him well. I quote it as it is given in Mr. Leyland's pages.†

* "Leyland," I., 266. † Ib., 268.

" He was," says Mr. Heaton, " blithe and gay, but at times appeared downcast and sad ; yet if the subject were some topic that he was acquainted with, or some author he loved, he would rise from his seat, and in beautiful language, describe the author's character, with a zeal and fluency I had never heard equalled. His talents were of a very exalted kind. I have heard him quote pieces from the bard of Avon, from Shelley, Wordsworth and Byron, as well as from Butler's 'Hudibras,' in such a manner as often made me wish I had been a scholar as he was. . . . He lent me books which I had never seen before, and was ever ready to give me information. His temper was always mild towards me. I shall never forget his love for the sublime and beautiful works of Nature, nor how he would tell of the lovely flowers and rare plants he had observed by the mountain stream and woodland rill. All these had excellencies for him ; and I have often heard him dilate on the sweet strains of the nightingale, and on the thoughts that bewitched him the first time he heard one."*

* " Leyland," I., p. 269.

While at Luddenden Foot Branwell made many local excursions up that lovely valley. He had friends in the neighburhood at Hebden Bridge, and we hear from Mr. Leyland that sometimes 'clerical visitors' called at his wooden shanty to hear his brilliant conversation. They invited him to their houses also, and it was while here that Branwell paid a visit to Manchester Cathedral. But these excursions drew him away from his proper duties; he did not attend as closely to his work as he ought to have done; frequently he left it in charge of his deputy; and he was undoubtedly careless in his accounts. The Company invited him to appear before them and explain these irregularities. They decided to terminate his engagement with them, and so, after two years of employment, ended Branwell's career as a railway clerk.

It was an ignominious ending, and it plunged him in the greatest gloom. He felt keenly the disgrace attached to his dismissal, all the more because it was such a disappointment to his family. He had supported himself for two years, however, and immediately began to look out for another situation. He applied to Mr. Grundy, but that gentleman did nothing for him, probably feeling convinced that business was the last thing for which his dreamy, volatile, poetical friend was fitted. But he answered in a friendly tone, suggesting he should try one of the professions. This meant the Church, and for the Church Branwell declared he had no mental qualification which might make him "cut a figure in its pulpits . . . save, perhaps, hypocrisy." But he goes on to say that Mr. James Montgomery and another literary gentleman, who had seen something of his work, advised him to "turn his attention to Literature." To this career, as we know, Branwell was much attracted already, though he did not take himself with any great seriousness as yet. He admits to Mr. Grundy that he has "little conceit of himself," but a great desire for activity. He was in fact infected with that fever of restlessness which seems to have burned alike in his veins and those of his sister Charlotte. In the months following his return to the Parsonage, we find Branwell solacing his weariness and enforced leisure with the writing of Poetry. To this year, early 1842, we may assign three of his best Sonnets: "On Landseer's Painting—The Shepherd's Chief Mourner"; "On the Callousness produced by Care"; and on "Peaceful Death and Painful Life."

He was in a condition of comparative loneliness at this time, as all his sisters were away from home, Anne teaching in a family who lived about twelve miles from York, and Charlotte and Emily at Brussels, in the establishment of M. Héger.

In September his aunt, Miss Branwell, suddenly became very ill. Branwell was fortunately at hand to do his utmost for her. She suffered terribly and only lived a fortnight. Branwell was unremitting in his attentions to her, but nothing could save her. It was while sitting under the shadow of this impending bereavement that Branwell wrote to his friend Grundy:—"I have had a long attendance at the death-bed of the Rev. Mr. Weightman, one of my dearest friends, and now I am attending at the death-bed of my aunt, who has been for twenty years as my mother. I expect her to die in a few hours. As my sisters are far from home, I have had much on my mind, and these things must serve as an apology for what was never intended as neglect of your friendship to us. I had meant not only to have written to you, but to the Rev. James Martineau, gratefully and sincerely acknowledging the receipt of his most kindly and truthful criticism—at least in advice, though too generous far in praise; but one sad ceremony must, I fear, be gone through first." A week later he writes to Mr. Grundy again :—" I am incoherent, I fear, but I have been waking two nights witnessing such agonizing suffering as I would not wish my worst enemy to endure: and I have now lost the guide and director of all the happy days connected with my childhood. I have suffered much sorrow since I last saw you at Haworth."*

Miss Branwell died on the 28th of October,

* Shorter, " The Brontës and Their Circle," p. 115.

1842, while all her nieces were away. She was buried before Emily and Charlotte were able to return. By the terms of her will, made as early as 1833, when Branwell was only a boy of fifteen, she left her little savings to her nieces, so once again we notice that it was not the sisters who were financially sacrificed. But even this bequest has been made an excuse for belabouring Branwell, whose supposed depravity at the age of fifteen has been the reason assigned by Mrs. Gaskell and Miss Robinson for his loss of benefit. Mr. Leyland displays a quite laudable indignation on the subject. "It is", he writes, "amazing that so much ignorance should have been displayed on a subject so easily capable of being correctly stated; but it is lamentable that this ignorance should have led the biographers of the Brontës by erroneous statements, to inflict additional and unmerited injury on Branwell."*

But to inflict injury on Branwell has by this time become, as I have already pointed out, a positive obsession with some of our Brontë writers, among whom Miss Sinclair is noticeably promi-

† "Leyland," XXXIII., p. 31-32.

nent. All her references to Branwell are made in a tone of almost heartless flippancy, and with a careless disregard for the facts of the case that is surprising in a writer of her distinction. She rivals Miss Robinson in prejudice, though with less excuse, for her predecessor had not access to the more recent material included in Mr. Leyland's volumes, which Miss Sinclair apparently finds it convenient to ignore, as, for example, when she remarks of this particular event, the death of Miss Branwell and the sudden recall of Emily and Charlotte from abroad :—" Then, in their first year of Brussels, their old Aunt, Miss Branwell, died. . . . Things were going badly and sadly at the Parsonage. Branwell was there drinking."* On the contrary, we know now how usefully and tenderly Branwell was employed, and there is not the remotest shadow of evidence for this cruel and uncalled for assertion. " Meanwhile ", writes Mrs. Gaskell, " they enjoyed their Christmas all together inexpressibly. Branwell was with them ; that was always a pleasure at this time." And so ended the year 1842.

* " Three Brontës," p. 25.

IV

"MUCH TRIBULATION"

AND now, we come to the last and most critical period of Branwell Brontë's life. In January, 1843, immediately after the events just detailed, he obtained another post, as tutor in Mr. Robinson's family at Thorp Green, in the neighbourhood of Boroughbridge and York, where his sister Anne was already installed as governess. For the next two and a half years, till the end of July, 1845, he retained this situation, obviously giving satisfaction to his employer. These years we may certainly regard as the happiest in Branwell's so far not too fortunate life, inasmuch as, for the first time in his experience, he was in daily contact with a woman of the most engaging charm and breeding, the like of whom, we may believe, he had never yet enjoyed the privilege of meeting. Mrs. Robinson was a woman of the world, who, without necessarily giving any thought to the matter, could hardly fail to attract the ardent admiration of an impressionable, inexperienced, poetic young man of twenty-five. She was his senior by about seventeen years, but judging from the impression she made on Branwell, we may conclude she was equally attractive in person and intellect. The comparative luxury and elegance of her surroundings lent her added grace and dignity. Probably they were thrown much together in consultation about her son's education, or in drawing lessons, sketching parties, walks up and down the alleys of the large secluded garden and the like, until the radiance of her graciousness and charm completely dazzled the young tutor. At first his feelings may have been those of a young troubadour toward his queen of love and beauty, a being elevated far above his reach, to whom it was out of the question that he should even aspire. But as the months grew into years and their intimacy increased, his feelings for the lady of his reverence became inflamed, until, little by little, whether encouraged by any response on her part or not, he fell hopelessly in love with her.

Branwell Brontë is by no means the first and only learned young clerk or poet who has fallen in love with a mistress far above him in fortune and position. The story is as old as the world. In manners, at least, and rich mental gifts Branwell was Mrs. Robinson's equal; knowing his own gifts and culture, it was not perhaps such "frantic folly," as Charlotte afterwards called it, to dream that one day he might win her for himself. Such apparently unequal yokings have often occurred, and have been justified by their success. But to fail in such daring aspiration—that is the danger; for to be repulsed, to be repudiated, is humiliation indeed.

Whether Mrs. Robinson had given Branwell the right to be her champion against her husband, who, he declared, did not treat her well, or whether the lady's affection for Branwell was a phantasy of his over-heated imagination, does not particularly matter to us now. What does matter is the deep love he bore her, a love which, whether returned or not, was to prove the direct and tragic cause of his complete undoing.

In the wholesale condemnation to which Branwell Brontë's mad passion for his employer's wife has given rise, the human element in him has scarcely been allowed fair play. We ought, before condemning him, to know just how far he may have been drawn on by the fancied appeal of a woman who was not particularly happy with her husband. We ought also, before con demning him, to reflect that he came of a wild-blooded Irish stock, that he was of Celtic, not Saxon, origin, possessing all the impulsive, ardent, poetic temperament of a race which has ever been noted for its gallantry to the gentler sex, a race that has never been remarkable for the phlegmatic control of its emotions. Branwell undoubtedly also possessed the weakness of disposition, combined with passionate ardour, which is easily allured by women, especially so cultivated, experienced and fascinating a creature as Mrs. Robinson proved herself to be. She may, perhaps unconsciously, have given him sufficient encouragement to lead him to suppose he had a particular place in her esteem : it is certain, at any rate, that the fantastically dreaming youth assumed that his devotion was returned. Little by little the passion grew in his soul till his whole being was devoured by the thought of her, and quite seriously, however foolishly, he looked forward to the time when she might be free, and he would be able to ask her hand in marriage. Whether the lady regarded herself as pledged to Branwell can never be known. Nor, in spite of Miss Sinclair's positive assurance on the subject,* has it ever been divulged how Branwell's attentions to his wife were made known to Mr. Robinson. All that we do know is that Branwell had just returned home for the midsummer vacation when he received a letter from his employer summarily dismissing him from his tutorship, and threatening him with the fullest exposure if he dared to hold any further communication with the family at Thorp Green.

This sudden and unexpected blow was almost too much for Branwell's sanity. Whatever was true or false in his love story, the agony and

* "The Three Brontës," p. 30.

humiliation of this abrupt dismissal was real enough. Such a passion as he had allowed to grow up in his heart and mind could not be eradicated or destroyed without tearing up the very roots of his being.

To his indignant family, however, it merely appeared fantastic or preposterous; Charlotte was shocked and angered beyond measure, the more so as the whole family were for a brief period the victims of his uncontrollable agitation, almost amounting to unreason. For a space of eleven nights, as he himself afterwards confided to a friend, he lay in " sleepless horror " until change of scene was imperative, and in the care of John Brown he went to Liverpool, whence he took boat for the Welsh coast.

The change was immediately beneficial. The beauty of the scenery brought peace once more to his troubled spirit—witness his poem, " Penmaenmawr ", written at this time. He returned composed and outwardly calm, determined to face his misery and live it down as best he might. Hope still animated him that possibly all was not lost, that some day he might marry the object of his devotion. Thus buoyed up, he continued some work which, he gives his friend Leyland to understand, he had begun some years previously, but to which he had not till now turned his serious attention. During the comparative leisure he had enjoyed at Thorp Green, a situation in which he was, to use his own expression, " so much the master ", Branwell had directed his thoughts to prose literature, and had projected and commenced a novel, of which he had compiled the first volume. Upon his return from Wales, he took up this task once more.

To this subject of Branwell's novel we shall presently return. For the moment we are merely concerned with mentioning it as one of the outstanding facts in Branwell's life, and to shew that his concentration on this piece of literary composition goes far to prove that, at this time at least, he was not the confirmed drunkard Mrs. Gaskell and others have made him out to be. His mental powers were indeed now at their zenith: of his brilliance, both now and to the last days of his life, Mr. Leyland insists that there can be no doubt. Indeed, it was during the few months following his return from Thorp Green that he produced, both in prose and verse, the finest work of his life.

Things were apparently going moderately well with him until the following spring, when, in May, 1846, he received the news of the death of Mr. Robinson, his late employer. This momentous incident raised his hopes to ecstacy, only, however, to dash them immediately to earth, for as he was about to set out at once with the expectation of again meeting the woman on the memory of whom he had been living for the past ten months, a messenger arrived bringing him the news that he could never see her again, inasmuch as the terms of Mr. Robinson's will absolutely precluded his widow's remarriage, except with loss of the estate.

Thus, deprived of all hope, Branwell's case was more desperate than before. In a letter to a friend, he writes: "Well, my dear sir, I have got my finishing stroke at last, and I feel stunned into marble by the blow. . . . It's hard work for me, dear sir; I would bear it, but my health is so bad that the body seems as if it could not bear the mental shock. . . . My appetite is lost, my nights are dreadful; and having nothing to do, makes me dwell on past scenes . . . till I would be glad if God would take me. In the next world I could not be worse than I am in this."*

If his summary dismissal from Thorp Green at the end of July, 1845, had sent Branwell reeling to the ropes, this gave him his knock-out blow. His health, which had been long undermined by frequent illnesses, now gave way, and his nervous system went to pieces. There seemed no hope for him anywhere, and no one to lend him a helping hand. Something could still have been done for him had the personality of his elder sister been other than it was, but her patience was exhausted, her pride outraged, and she made it clear on all sides, both in the family and out of it, that she took no further interest in him.

Since the time of Branwell's return from his railway appointment it seems as if his family had

* "Leyland," II, p. 147.

gradually begun to lose faith in his capacity to achieve that brilliant career to which they, no less than he himself, were looking forward. Charlotte, in particular, was intolerant of failure. And though Branwell's apparent success at Thorp Green had once more stimulated her interest in his prospects, his sudden dismissal in the summer of 1845, added to his own temporary loss of self-control, seems to have completely alienated her sympathy from this formerly cherished brother.

Nothing is more ruthless than love which has turned to hate, and Charlotte confesses in one of her letters to Ellen Nussey, that she was "a hearty hater."* She was moreover possessed of a hard vein of biting sarcasm which, combined with an explosive temper when crossed, must have made her, for the inmates of the Parsonage, "gey ill to live wi'." It may be said that her attitude towards Branwell was natural enough, that is, for those whose standard is measured by her criterion. She had hoped and planned for her brother all his life through; she had been, we can

* "Life," p. 86.

believe, his constant spur to action; she had seen his marked ability; she was conscious of his gifts; and now she was suffering from the exasperation, the mortification of seeing those gifts and abilities, as she thought, wasted, thrown away in the pursuit of an infatuation which she could only term "frantic folly". Her endurance and patience were at an end. She had her own work, her own career to attend to, and the care of her father. There was not room in her heart for both her own consuming ambition and concentration on this failure of a brother. Branwell must go. And with the final overthrow and extinction, so she believed, of his prospects, she swept him out of her path.

Searching Charlotte's correspondence at this time and during the next three years of Branwell's life, we glean not a single word of love or pity for her brother: nothing but ringing contempt. For his intervals of self-control and temperance she gives him no credit, remarking sarcastically, that he is "forced to abstain." When her friend Ellen Nussey is about to visit them, Charlotte assures her that she need not fear any incivility from Branwell, and sarcastically adds, "on the contrary, he will be as smooth as oil."* Yes, assuredly Charlotte was a good hater.

And yet, Charlotte Brontë was what by all recognized standards would be described as a fine character; she was brave, upright, honourable, and in the main, just. But she possessed the defects of her almost Roman temperament in a marked degree. The honour of the family name and the pursuit of her own personal ambition were dearer to her than the saving of her own brother—if indeed he could be saved. She had in her, too, not merely the indifference of the pagan to the misery of the world's weaklings, but also a touch of that fanatical strain which formerly produced martyrs or great reformers; of that ascetic severity characteristic of a Conrad or a Calvin. She had much righteousness of vision, but little tolerance for wrongdoers. The sinner must be shewn his sin, reasoned with certainly, but if he gave no visible promise of amendment,

* Shorter, "The Brontë Circle," p. 125.

he must be cut off both from sympathy and intercourse. Her disposition had in it something of the harsh fierceness of that bitter north-easter, which made the shivering traveller hug his cloak rather than discard it; she had nothing of the sun in her nature, the all-loving, all-forgiving sun, shining alike on the evil and the good, nothing of the tender gentleness of the rain, falling like the tears of God's pity alike on the just and unjust. There was no halting between two opinions with Charlotte; everything was either black or white, right or wrong; and in her denunciation of wrong she was pitiless. Poor Branwell was, as we know, wrong in many ways. We can believe that she may have reasoned with him at first, but when in spite of her remonstrances he went again astray, when he fell, not once but many times, and again and again, it was too much for her patience; she was not one of those who could forgive her brother unto seventy times seven. Seven times was more than enough for her, and if after this he continued in his evil ways, then she felt justified in gathering up her garments and passing him by. It is related by Miss Robinson, I know not on what authority—unless that of Miss Nussey—that for two years Charlotte never spoke to her brother.

One pauses to wonder at the temerity that dares to judge and punish the shortcomings of a sister or brother, whose case, but for the accident of birth, might have been one's own. How easy for those secure on land to condemn the distracted master of the vessel, assailed at once by the winds and waves of material ill-fortune, weakened by anxiety and fever, bound it may be by his mutinous crew of wild passions, when he loses his grasp of the rudder and his ship drifts helplessly upon the rocks! I am inclined to believe that Charlotte's attitude was a dominating factor in her brother's life. Hitherto he had not wholly forfeited her good opinion, but now that she deserted him, he felt himself like a rudderless ship, like Cowper's hopeless "Castaway".

To know that he had not merely lost the woman he loved so deeply, and lost her for ever, but that with her, and because of her, he had lost the respect of his high-minded sister, was to feel that he was indeed at the end of all things, and henceforth he gave himself up to despair. Charlotte's scorn lashed him as with scorpions, her eyes darted lightnings of contempt that blasted his soul. He himself, in a conversation with a friend, refers to an occasion when he was terribly cut up by one of his sister's rebuffs: "One of the Sunday-school girls fell sick, and they were afraid she would not live. I went to see the poor little thing," he said, "sat with her half an hour, and read a psalm to her and a hymn at her request. I felt very like praying with her too," he added, his voice trembling with emotion, "but, you see, I was not good enough. . . . I came away with a heavy heart, and went straight home, where I fell into melancholy musings. I wanted somebody to cheer me. . . . Charlotte observed my depression, and asked what ailed me. So I told her. She looked at me with a look I shall never forget—if I live to be a hundred years old. . . . It wounded me as if someone had struck me a blow in the mouth. It involved ever so many things in it. It was a dubious look. It ran over me, questioning and examining, as if I had been a wild beast. It said, 'Did my ears deceive me or did I hear aright?' And then came the painful, baffled expression, which was worse than all. It said, 'I wonder if that's true?'"*

Charlotte's inward knowledge of her own lapse, her secret passion for Monsieur Héger, for which she scourged herself night and day, instead of making her more tender to her brother's fault, possibly aggravated her indignation: she had known what it was to suffer the pangs of frustrated passion, but she had burnt out the plague-spot in her flesh. Let him do likewise. Whether this was her argument or not, the fact remains that after a time she utterly repudiated her brother, and made no further attempts to draw him out of the Slough of Despond into which he had fallen.

Charlotte's behaviour to her brother at this time of his greatest need is the one fault in her

* Quoted in an article by Mr. G. S. Phillips in "The Mirror," for 1872. Printed by Leyland, II., p. 127.

otherwise blameless life, which it is difficult to condone. Branwell Brontë was in some respects a wrong-doer, but he was really a very sick man. For the last two years of his life he was suffering from extreme bodily weakness, and great mental distress. He was a victim of neurasthenia, a disease not then understood or recognized, but which is carefully treated in our more enlightened day. With subjects in the condition of Branwell Brontë it is above all things vital never to let them lose their self-respect, never to let them see that you have lost faith in their powers of recovery. Firmness and loving-kindness will work miracles in apparently hopeless cases. A well-known medical writer, Dr. Brown, who has published a book on the subject, describes cases very similar to Branwell's sufferings.*

After the "emotional shock" of his dismissal from Thorp Green and Mrs. Robinson's later repudiation of him, we may fairly conclude

*"Suggestion and Mental Analysis," by William Brown, M.A., M.D. (Oxon), D.Sc., etc. (University of London Press, Ltd.) 1922.

he was much more a subject for a nursing home than for a penitentiary. The critical atmosphere of the Parsonage was hostile to him ; no nursing of nervous disorders there, no recognition of them even. In the few comments which Charlotte makes upon her brother, she always conveys the impression that she had not a grain of sympathy for him, not the faintest understanding of his case, nor any wish to understand it.

The attitude of his father and the other sisters was, from all we can gather, more forbearing than that of Charlotte. Anne, who had been with him at Thorp Green, and who must have known a good deal about the relations between Branwell and Mrs. Robinson, refers somewhat enigmatically to what she had seen, and adds, very temperately, that her brother " has had much tribulation and ill-health." She also expresses the hope that " he will get better and do better in future." Emily Brontë, at the same date, July 30th, 1845, writes : " We are all in decent health . . . with the exception of Branwell, who, I hope, will be better and do better hereafter." These respective opinions were written, it will be noticed, almost immediately after Branwell's first breakdown, and with full knowledge of all that had occurred. This almost tender attitude is in sharp contrast with Charlotte's resentful harshness, and, as regards Emily Brontë, is of the most momentous importance, as I hope presently to show. Emily is supposed to have been his favourite sister, though all his life he had been dominated by the strong nature of Charlotte. It was Emily who now took him to her heart, and who hung over him through the remaining three years of his broken life with all the tenderness of a mother.

In August of this year, 1846, Charlotte went with her father to Manchester, where he was operated on for cataract. Branwell shared his sisters' anxiety as to the result of the operation, as we know from a letter to Mr. Grundy, in which he says: "My father, too, is quite blind, and from such causes literary pursuits have become matters I have no heart to wield."

Emily and Anne remained at the Parsonage with Branwell during the month of Charlotte's

Haworth Parsonage in the time of the Brontës.

absence, and they apparently got on with much comfort together. It was probably at this time that Mr. Grundy paid a last visit to Haworth Parsonage, and met Emily. To this important visit I shall presently have occasion to refer. By the help of his old friend, Mr. Grundy, Branwell still hoped to receive some post in connection with the Leeds railway, but his application met with no success. Continual failure in every direction was very depressing to his spirits, already in a drooping condition. Even had he been successful, it is doubtful if his health, at this time particularly wretched, would have permitted him to undertake serious daily duties. But, while he continued to look out for employment, he occupied himself in writing poetry, though he confesses to his correspondents, Mr. Grundy and Mr. Leyland, that he feels too physically prostrate to attempt any big literary undertaking in prose.

We can hardly accept Charlotte's statement that her brother was totally unaware of his sisters' activities at this time, as, when, on some occasion of Charlotte's having written to a publisher and received no reply, Mrs. Gaskell mentions that "she consulted her brother as to what could be the reason for the prolonged silence. He at once set it down to her not having enclosed a postage stamp in her letter. She accordingly wrote again, to repair her former omission and apologize for it."* The discrepancy suggests that Charlotte's memory was not quite trustworthy, as might easily be the case after the lapse of years.

Branwell's health now rapidly declined, although Charlotte fiercely and persistently refused to acknowledge the truth. She sneered at his professions of weakness, though, from the accounts that have come down to us, it is obvious that he was unfit for any employment requiring physical vigour. In every reference to his illnesses she attributes them to nothing but his own fault. She could not or would not see that the man's spirit had sustained a mortal blow; that he desperately needed cheering, that he was abandoned and terribly lonely, that for some reason or other he was physically wasting away; that he had

* "Life," p. 222-23.

neither the mental nor physical strength to fight further, and was in no condition to stand up against the raking fire of her illimitable scorn; that he was in fact dying, dying on his feet, dying from consumption brought on by self-neglect, despair and a broken heart.

In every biography of his sisters we hear of Branwell's drinking habits. It is undeniable that he was fond of conviviality, which at times—but only at times—ran to excess. Nothing is gained by any attempt to exonerate him from this deplorable and unfortunate weakness. His ancestry and careless upbringing were predisposing influences, and the habits of his contemporaries offered no example of restraint. In the generation immediately preceding his own, heavy drinking had been the recognized accomplishment of a gentleman, a wit, or a man about town. The Elizabethans had set the fashion; the frequenters of the Coffee Houses had followed it; even the reputable Addison is said to have tippled, and certainly Steele, Fox, Goldsmith, Sheridan, Burns and Byron were all notoriously hard drinkers.

Charles Lamb was no exception, and frequently cursed his wretched drinking habits, which, on his own admission, contributed to his sister's mental disturbance. But Branwell Brontë was born in an age when the first recoil was beginning to be felt against these wild, carousing habits. To frequent an inn except as a traveller began to be taken as a sign of depravity, and it was the disgrace attached by Charlotte to her brother's evening visits to the "Black Bull" in the village that made her so bitter towards him.

Let it then be admitted at once, freely and without argument, that Branwell Brontë often drank heavily, and perhaps at times took opium. What I am concerned to dispute is that he was never the wholly degraded or habitual drunkard that his detractors would make him out. Here we have the evidence of Mr. Leyland and other reputable people who knew him personally. He had, says Mr. Leyland, long periods of temperance. At its worst, his drinking was more the indulgence of a convivial habit than anything else. It was apparently his only vice, and, deplorable as it might be, it bore the character of weakness rather than criminal misdemeanour.

In defence of Branwell it may be pleaded that all through his life he had few chances such as come to others. At the very first, as we have seen, when, buoyant with hope and inspiration, he set out to do great things in London, his prospects were immediately blighted, chiefly by lack of funds to pursue an art student's career. He had no money spent on him except during the few months of art tuition at Bradford. The only fund that might have provided him with a university education or other start in life was raided by Charlotte when she persuaded her aunt to finance her education and Emily's at the Héger's Brussels pensionnat.

Miss Sinclair is wide of the mark when she talks about the sisters going out as governesses in order that Branwell might pursue a glorious career. When Charlotte went to Roe Head as governess Emily went with her as a pupil, and was presently followed by Anne, and it was in all probability to help to educate her sisters, not

Branwell, that she volunteered her services to Miss Wooler. Nothing was spent on Branwell other than the week's expenses in London, and some painting lessons at Bradford for which his aunt probably paid. When Emily went for six months as a teacher in a school at Halifax, Branwell was already getting commissions for portraits at Bradford, and keeping himself. When after 1839 Anne and Charlotte took further short spells of teaching, Branwell was tutoring at Mr. Postlethwaite's, and immediately after that he went for two years as railway clerk at Sowerby Bridge and Luddenden Foot. This disposes of the suggestion that the sisters were out earning a hard living as governesses while he was doing nothing. The whole suggestion is not merely ridiculous, but malicious. "Our debts will be paid off," writes Emily in her secret letter to Anne, dated July, 1841. These debts Miss Sinclair has the hardihood, in face of known facts, to suggest were "probably Branwell's."* They had nothing to do with Branwell. He was at this time earning

* "The Three Brontës," p. 23.

his own living on the railway. What Emily is referring to, if Miss Sinclair would take the trouble to read the context, are those they would have incurred in founding that "pleasant and flourishing seminary" of their dreams, which Emily has just mentioned in the preceding sentence. But, as Miss Sinclair accepts all her predecessors' attitude towards Branwell, any stick is good enough to aim a blow, whether merited or not, on the old woman's principle that "if he didn't deserve that particular whipping he soon would do."

There was one occasion on which they had to pay some of their brother's debts, in the winter of 1846, but Branwell was no idle acceptor of gifts, for, in a letter to Mr. Leyland, he expresses the wish that Mr. —— would send him his bill, "and the moment that I receive my outlaid cash, or any sum that falls into my hands, I shall settle it." This was probably some tailor's bill which he had incurred while he was at the Robinsons', with the full expectation of meeting it out of his future salary, and which, owing to his unexpected dismissal, he was obviously unable to meet. It was unfortunate, of course. The Sheriff's officer arrived; Charlotte bitterly resented the disgrace, and promptly wrote off and told her friend Ellen Nussey all about it.

In all her letters to this friend, when Charlotte has nothing in particular to relate, she finds occasion to say something disagreeable about her brother. Do we impart the failings and weaknesses of those we love even to the nearest and dearest of our friends? But Charlotte went even farther: she told her old school-mistress, Miss Wooler, about her brother's failings. For this there can have been no necessity. Miss Wooler was not likely to visit Haworth, as Ellen Nussey was, and the only deduction we can draw is that Charlotte was unable to write a letter without detailing to her correspondents her own sufferings and all she had to put up with. It was assuredly Charlotte who was the egoist of the family. Had she loved Branwell she would have suffered more silently for his sake, instead of blazoning his unhappy weakness to every intimate correspondent. Miss Nussey had known Branwell from a boy, and as late as the winter of 1842-3, messages were being exchanged between them through the medium of Charlotte's letters. After 1845, however, Charlotte evidently decided that Ellen's interest in her brother must be checked, and, by her continual report of his delinquencies, she effectually wrecked his image in her friend's mind. Long before this, however, it had become evident, from Branwell's manner, that he had become completely absorbed in an entirely different personality.

The following letter to his friend Leyland, written some time about the close of the year 1846, or, more probably, in the opening of 1847, gives such a vivid picture of Branwell's mental and physical condition that I transcribe it in full:

"My DEAR SIR,

I am going to write a scrawl, for the querulous egotism of which I must entreat your mercy; but, when I look upon my past, present and future, and then into my own self, I find much, however unpleasant, that yearns for utterance.

This last week an honest and kindly friend has warned me that concealed hopes about one lady should be given up, let the effort to do so cost what it may. He is the ——, and was commanded by ——, M.P. for ——, to return me, unopened, a letter which I addressed to —— and which the lady was not permitted to see. She, too, surrounded by powerful persons who hate me like Hell, has sunk into religious melancholy, believes that her weight of sorrow is God's punishment, and hopelessly resigns herself to her doom. God only knows what it does cost and will, hereafter, cost me, to tear from my heart and remembrance the thousand recollections that rush upon me at the thought of four years gone by. Like ideas of sunlight to a man who has lost his sight, they must be bright phantoms not to be realized again. I had reason to hope that ere very long I should be the husband of a lady whom I loved best in the world, and with whom, in more than competence, I might live at leisure to try to make myself a name in the world of posterity, without being pestered by the small but countless botherments, which, like mosquitoes, sting us in the world of workday toil. That hope and herself are gone—she to wither into patiently pining decline, it to make room for drudgery, falling on one now ill-fitted to bear it. That ill-fittedness rises from causes which I find myself able partially to overcome, had I bodily strength; but, with the want of that, and with the presence of daily lacerated nerves, the task is not easy. I have been in truth too much petted through life, and, in my last situation, I was so much master, and gave myself so much up to enjoyment, that now, when the cloud of ill-health and adversity has come upon me, it will be a disheartening job to work myself up again, through a new life's battle, from the position of five years ago, to that from which I have been compelled to retreat with heavy loss and no gain. My army stands now where it did then, but mourning the slaughter of Youth, Health, Hope and both mental and physical elasticity.

The last two losses are, indeed, important to one who once built his hopes of rising in the world on the possession of them. Noble writings, works of art, music or poetry, now, instead of rousing my imagination, cause a whirlwind of blighting sorrow that sweeps over my mind with unspeakable dreariness; and, if I sit down and try to write, all ideas that used to come clothed in sunlight now press round me in funereal black; for really every pleasurable excitement that I used to know has changed to insipidity or pain.

I shall never be able to realize the too sanguine hopes of my friends, for at twenty-nine I am a thoroughly old man, mentally, and bodily, far more indeed than I am willing to express. God knows I do not scribble like a poetaster when I quote Byron's terribly truthful words:

> No more—no more—oh! never more on me
> The freshness of the heart shall fall like dew,
> Which, out of all the lovely things we see,
> Extracts emotions beautiful and new!

I used to think that if I could have, for a week, the free range of the British Museum—the library included—I could feel as though I were placed for seven days in Paradise; but now, really, dear sir, my eyes would rest upon the Elgin marbles, the Egyptian saloon, and the most treasured columns, like the eyes of a dead codfish. My rude, rough acquaintances here ascribe my unhappiness solely to causes produced by my sometimes irregular life, because they have known no other pains than those resulting from excess or want of ready cash. They do not know that I would sooner want a shirt than want a springy mind, and that my total want of happiness, were I to step into York Minster now, would be far, far worse than their want of a hundred pounds when they might happen to need it; and that, if a dozen glasses or a bottle of wine drives off their cares, such cures only make me outwardly passable in company, but never drive off mine. I know only that it is time for me to be something, when I am nothing, that my father cannot have long to live, and that, when he dies, my evening, which is already twilight, will become night; that I shall then have a constitution still so strong that it will keep me years in torture and despair, when I should every hour pray that I might die.

I know that I am avoiding, while I write, one greatest cause of my utter despair; but, by G——, sir, it is nearly too bitter for me to allude to it. (Here follow a number of references to the subject, which are omitted by Mr. Leyland.) To no one living have I said what I now say to you, and I should not bother yourself with my incoherent account did I not believe that you would be able to understand something of what was meant—though not all, sir; for he who is without hope, and knows that his clock is at twelve at night, cannot communicate his feelings to one who finds his at twelve at noon."*

The importance of this letter is great, because it is first-hand evidence, and because it shows us his utterly listless, hopeless and dejected condition, with no interest in any work of art or literature, his own or others', outside his narrowly confined horizon of vision. He was the

* "Leyland," II., p. 177.

victim of one idea—his frustrated passion for Mrs. Robinson. It also shows, without the possibility of doubt, the shockingly weak condition of health and spirits into which he had fallen. He was surely a subject for pity rather than for the scorn and derision with which his elder sister regarded him.

The winter of 1846–7 was a particularly trying one, and both Branwell and Mr. Brontë had influenza and bronchial trouble. In the following May, Charlotte invited her friend Miss Nussey to visit them, a thing she would never have done had Branwell's conduct been all that his biographers have tried to make out. He was depressed, but still trying to employ his time with writing, chiefly poetry, a poem "Morley Hall" in particular, for his friend Leyland. This may have been a commission, given him in kindness partly to distract his mind. He never ceased to prosecute enquiries as to "situations suitable to me, whereby I could have a voyage abroad." These, however, came to nothing, though a voyage south would greatly have benefited both mind and body. During this year—1847—which proved a terrible one for his failing health, he wrote another poem, significantly called "The End of All." One more poem, however, was attempted after this, but remained unfinished. Its title was "Percy Hall."

It is obvious that, to the very last, Branwell retained his gifts of poetic expression and a graphic power of personal narration which, his hearers relate, was nothing short of marvellous. Mr. Leyland affirms that "he himself could endorse" all that Mr. Phillips says about Branwell's brilliancy of intellect at this time. Mr. Phillips admits he was much altered in appearance during the latter part of their acquaintance, but goes on to say, "if he had altered in the same direction mentally, as his biographer says he had, then he must have been a man of immense and brilliant intellect. For, I have rarely heard more eloquent and thoughtful discourse, flashing so brightly with random jewels of wit, and made sunny and musical with poetry, than that which flowed from his lips during the evenings I passed with him at the 'Black Bull,' in the village of Haworth. His figure was very slight, and he had, like his sister Charlotte, a superb forehead. But, even when pretty deep in his cups, he had not the slightest appearance of the sot that Mrs. Gaskell says he was. 'His great tawny mane,' meaning thereby the hair of his head, was, it is true, somewhat dishevelled; but, apart from this, he gave no sign of intoxication. His eye was as bright and his features were as animated as they very well could be; and, moreover, his whole manner gave indication of intense enjoyment."

The spring and summer of 1848 were wild, wet and unfavourable to one like Branwell, suffering from chronic bronchitis, and "marasmus," a consumptive wasting-away, arising from hereditary tendency, chill, and neglect of food, as well as from mental agony and the effects of irregular life. His family do not seem to have observed him very closely. On the 28th of July, Charlotte writes: "His constitution seems much shattered. Papa and sometimes all of us have sad nights with him. He sleeps most of the day, and consequently will lie awake at night. But has not every house its trial ?"

This is Charlotte's only comment on the desperate condition of her dying brother. He did not trouble them many weeks longer: on the morning of Sunday, the 24th of September, he died with tragic suddenness, after having been confined to bed only for a single day.

Charlotte, writing to a friend on the 9th of October, gives a short account of his last hours, and goes on to say: "A deep conviction that he rests at last, rests well, after his brief, erring, suffering, feverish life, fills and quiets my mind now. The final separation, the spectacle of his pale corpse gave me more acute bitter pain than I could have imagined. Till the last hour comes, we never know how much we can forgive, pity, regret a near relative. All his vices were and are nothing now. We remember only his woes."

How much more helpful to Branwell, could his sister Charlotte have pitied and forgiven him a little earlier in his lifetime. It was rather late in the day to remember his woes when he was dead.

V

WUTHERING HEIGHTS—BY EMILY ?

WE have heard the brief chronicle of the promise of genius cramped by ill-health, crushed by misfortune, yet constantly putting forth buds of rare beauty and vitality. Is it possible that any valuable fruit was produced, unknown to contemporaries, overlooked or neglected by biographers, or wrongly attributed to another as a miracle ?

It is now a matter of common knowledge to Brontë students that Branwell did claim to have written a work which, though published anonymously in his lifetime, only some eight months in fact before his untimely death, made no stir in the literary world either then or for many years after. This work was the novel, " Wuthering Heights," which has long been assigned to his sister Emily, chiefly, if not entirely, upon the evidence of Charlotte Brontë's " Preface and Biographical Memoir of her Sisters," issued with the edition of 1850. Charlotte made her statement, without doubt, in absolute good faith, completely believing that what she affirmed was the truth of the matter. There can be no doubt of this. She had probably never heard a word about any claim entered by her brother. A claim was made privately in a declaration to his friend, Mr. Grundy, and subsequently published by that gentleman in a volume of personal "Recollections" issued in the year 1879, long after Branwell, Emily and Charlotte were dead, so that there was no one left who could either confirm or refute it.

The matter dates from a visit of Mr. Grundy's to Haworth Parsonage, probably in the summer of 1846, when Charlotte was at Manchester with her father, and Branwell, Emily and Anne were left at home together. Mr. Grundy writes as follows: "One very important statement which he (Branwell) made to me throws some light upon a question which I observe has long vexed the critics, that is, the authorship of 'Wuthering Heights.' . . . It is well-nigh incredulous that a book so marvellous in its strength, and in the dissection of the most morbid passions of diseased minds, could have been written by a young girl like Emily, Brontë, who never saw much of the world, or knew much of mankind, and whose studies of life and character, if they are her own, must have been chiefly evolved from her own imagination. Patrick Brontë declared to me, and what his sister said bore out the assertion, that he wrote a great portion of 'Wuthering Heights' himself. Indeed, it is impossible for me to read that story without meeting with many passages which I feel certain must have come from his pen. The weird fancies of diseased genius with which he used to entertain me in our long talks at Luddenden Foot re-appear in the pages of the novel, and I am inclined to believe that the very plot was his invention rather than his sister's."*

Now, this claim of Branwell's, made, be it observed, when the novel was still going the round of the publishers, and, so far, without success, indeed often with nothing better than "an

* Francis H. Grundy, "Pictures of the Past," (Griffith & Farran,) 1879, p. 80.

ignominious and abrupt dismissal," with not a shadow of intimation of its future celebrity or of the genius that would be ascribed to its author; this in no way braggart claim, has been made "the whole head and front of his offending." Had he never made it, his shade would assuredly have been allowed to rest in obscurity and mediocrity. Having made it, however, and the claim having been subsequently published by Mr. Grundy, it could not be overlooked by those who had made themselves the passionate partisans of Emily's authorship. The hunt was now up, and the pursuers were determined to be satisfied with nothing short of the complete extirpation of Branwell Brontë. His character must be stained with the darkest colours; nothing bad enough could be invented about him; he was to be exposed as a bragging liar, a drunkard, an opium-eater; in short, a man so degraded, so lost to every sense of decent feeling that no reliance could be placed on any declaration of his, least of all upon the "preposterous statement," as Mr. Clement Shorter calls it, "that he wrote 'Wuthering Heights.'"

Yet, if Branwell Brontë was such a wretched creature as the biographers make out, why trouble about him at all? If his claim is actually so "preposterous," if his literary capacity is so completely negligible, why should the discussion of Branwell occupy so important a place in all the Brontë literature? What, in short, is the cause of all this feverish desire to "suppress" him running through all the pages of Miss Mary F. Robinson's monograph on Emily Brontë; through much of Miss May Sinclair's book on the same subject; and through Mr. Clement Shorter's work on the "Brontës and their Circle"? Can it be due to an uneasy feeling in their minds that Branwell's declaration of authorship may not be easily got rid of? Can it be the dread lest Emily Brontë's reputation as the author of this great novel is trembling in the balance? And is it then in order to safeguard the interests of Emily that one and all they never cease, on any occasion open to them, to dig up and insult her brother's ethical and literary remains?

If they are so sure about Emily's reputation,

if it is really secure and removed beyond all dispute, why all this vituperation of poor Branwell? Why not let him rest in well-deserved obscurity, why not inscribe "Pobre" over his tombstone and let him be? Is it that, having committed themselves irrevocably to the championship of Emily, they are ashamed to draw back?

Even if she did not write "Wuthering Heights," they have nothing to fear: she has renown enough without it. Let us therefore try to sift the evidence, openly and without prejudice, in the fair court of Public Opinion, not impatiently prejudging the case and anticipating the verdict along with the impassioned admirers of Emily Brontë. Because we love Emily—and the present writer will yield to no one in admiration of her—because of that very admiration and a certain prepossession in her favour, we have to be the more careful to avoid the bias that would make our verdict accord with our secret wishes.

Whether Emily Brontë wrote "Wuthering Heights" or not, she would still remain what she is, one of the most remarkable and lofty-minded women the world has ever known. Her "Poems" would still entitle her to fame, though perhaps not to the extended reputation she has received as a novelist.

Leaving these generalities, let us marshal such facts as are available for the fair examination of the question. This examination involves four particular enquiries. What further evidence is there, apart from Mr. Grundy's statement, of Branwell's claim to and qualification for the authorship? How did it come to pass that Charlotte knew nothing about her brother's claim? On what grounds did she so confidently found her assertion of Emily's authorship? What were the evidences of Emily's authorship, and her qualifications for the work?

It will be convenient to consider these points in a reverse order, first laying before the reader all that is certain and accepted as regards Emily's connection with it, including an estimate of her particular capacity for writing it, together with Charlotte's available information; leaving the discussion of Branwell's claim for a later page.

All we know about Emily's presumptive authorship is that when, in the winter of 1845-6, Charlotte was urging each of her sisters to "prepare" a novel for publication, to be offered along with one she herself had written, Emily "produced" this book, "Wuthering Heights," to be sent to the publishers, *not* as the work of Emily Brontë, but of "Ellis Bell," the pseudonym which had been already assigned to her in connection with the publication of the joint book of Poems which Charlotte had already given to the Press. The book was presumably in her hand-writing and consequently passed for hers, but there is no evidence that it had been shown to her other sisters in instalments, or discussed between them "chapter by chapter," as some critics have averred. We have Charlotte's definite statement in her "Biographical Introduction," made with special reference to this work, that for some years they had "discontinued" their earlier habit of intercommunication and consultation.

This novel, when read by Charlotte or aloud to her, not merely surprised, but completely astounded her. It fell on her ears like a clap of thunder. She was absolutely horrified. She admits that she "shuddered" as she listened, and "the mere hearing of certain vivid and fearful scenes banished sleep by night, and disturbed mental peace by day."* It seemed almost inconceivable to her that her quiet, retiring sister could have created anything so apparently alien to her own disposition, character and limited experience. The whole relationship between Emily and the book which passed ostensibly as hers was a puzzle and a problem to Charlotte; but, however mystified or curious Charlotte might be, Emily never enlightened her sister as to what had prompted her to such a strange work. She remained silent and immutable as a sphinx, or merely put Charlotte's complaints aside as smacking of "affectation." Obviously she would not discuss the work in any way, at least not with Charlotte.

Upon its publication eighteen months later, in December, 1847, we find Charlotte, in a letter to Mr. Williams, the reader for Messrs. Smith &

* Preface to 1850 edition of "Wuthering Heights."

Elder, half apologizing for the contrast between the "refined" poetry of "Ellis Bell" and the prose of "Wuthering Heights"—a prose which, she says, "breaks forth in scenes which shock more than they attract."* The book had a bad reception, and a bad press. The author was universally supposed to be a man, and a very coarse and brutal one. At length it began to be suggested that "it was an earlier and ruder attempt by the same pen that produced 'Jane Eyre.'" This was in the summer of 1848, about two months before Branwell's death, when the book had been published only about six months. Charlotte was much upset, and determined to put the matter right with her London publishers by taking her sisters with her to convince Mr. Williams and Mr. Smith of their separate identity. Here then was an opportunity for Emily to proclaim herself the veritable author of the book. But what happened?

She would not, and did not go.

None the less, Mr. Clement Shorter, in his eager

* Letter to W. S. Williams, quoted "The Brontës and their Circle," p. 146.

anxiety to establish Emily's authorship, is determined that she must be "got" there, and accordingly makes the astonishing blunder of putting Emily's name instead of Anne's in connection with this visit.* Miss Sinclair avoids this pitfall, but professes to account for Emily's refusal to prefer her claim in person by attributing it to her pride and a superb indifference.

But Emily went even further than this. Not only did she refuse to make a personal claim of authorship, but, on Charlotte's return, she evidently took her very sharply to task for making unwarranted assumptions on her behalf, namely, for telling Messrs. Smith and Williams that there were "three" sisters who were authors. Mrs. Chadwick has drawn attention to this point. In reference to the authorship of "Wuthering Heights," she says: "It was sent out as the work of Ellis Bell, and only as such was she determined that it should be known."† The letter Charlotte

* "Brontës and their Circle," p. 6. A Brontë Chronology.

† "In the Footsteps of the Brontës," p. 325.

was immediately pressed by Emily to write in correction of this error is given by Mr. Shorter, and I here quote the part to which Mrs. Chadwick refers: "Permit me to caution you not to speak of my sisters when you write to me. I mean, do not use the word in the plural. Ellis Bell will not endure to be alluded to under any other appellation than the *nom-de-plume.* I committed a grand error in betraying his identity to you and Mr. Smith. It was inadvertent—the words 'we are three sisters' escaped me before I was aware. I regretted the avowal the moment I had made it; I regret it bitterly now, for I find it is against every feeling and intention of Ellis Bell."*

This is startling evidence indeed. What is the obvious deduction from this strong, almost angry protest, which Charlotte was constrained to make on behalf of Emily?

Might it not be that Emily, who, as Charlotte tells us, was incapable of "trickery", would not for one moment allow it to be either presumed or established that she, Emily Brontë, was to be

* "The Brontës and their Circle," p. 361.

identified with "Ellis Bell"? And, what for our present purpose is even more significant, we find her insisting that this same "Ellis," who is not to be identified with herself, is not to be assumed to be one of the "three sisters." What then is the inference? Is it not clear from these remarkable stipulations of Emily's, which we may believe worried Charlotte not a little, that Emily was concealing another person's authorship under her pseudonym? That by obliging Charlotte to write this letter she went as far as she possibly could in disclaiming the work for herself? That, although she hated and was incapable of "trickery" in the accepted sense of that word, she was nevertheless bound in some mysterious, secret way not to reveal the real authorship of the book?

Yet, if she was concealing someone else's authorship, whose could it be? She hotly repudiates, through Charlotte, the idea that "Ellis Bell" is either herself or one of the Brontë "sisters": who then was "Ellis Bell"? And what "intention" of Emily's was violated by coupling this pseudonym with her own name?

Was "Ellis Bell" Branwell Brontë? And was this "intention" of Emily's her endeavour to conceal his authorship of "Wuthering Heights"? And why should she conceal it?

Before entering into the discussion of these exciting questions, it is first necessary to deal with Emily's own capacity for writing the book, and to enquire closely into her known literary activities at the very period when she produced "Wuthering Heights," and handed it to Charlotte for publication. This will take us back to the summer of 1845, and more particularly to the month of July, when Branwell had just received his dismissal from Thorp Green, and Charlotte had already begun to turn her thoughts to the rôle of author.

Students of the Brontës will have noticed their peculiar love of "secrets"; their plays were often thus described. "Best plays mean secret plays," writes Charlotte in 1829.* They maintained this idea of secrecy no doubt in several writings,

* "Life," p. 55. "These are our three great plays that are not kept secret."

but we meet with it notably in another instance, at a much later date, when one might suppose they had outgrown the youthful fancies which had first prompted it. In this case it was two secret letters, one to be written from Anne to Emily, at the end of every four years, and one from Emily to Anne at the same time. Both letters were to be indited and locked up, and finally opened on Emily's birthday at the close of the appointed period. This little piece of intimacy between the sisters Anne and Emily, who were especially devoted to one another, does not seem to have been extended to Charlotte, who probably knew nothing about it. But Emily was full of fun, and enjoyed a specially private mystery between herself and one she tenderly loved. By an unprecedented piece of literary good fortune, Mr. Clement Shorter has chanced upon these brief little records for the years 1841 and 1845. Emily's birthday being on the 30th of July, they are dated accordingly.

In these letters there is a further secret, a private literary partnership between Anne and

Emily in the story of some imaginary people called by the writers, "The Gondialand." In 1841 Emily writes to Anne: "The Gondialand are at present in a threatening state, but there is no open rupture as yet. All the princes and princesses of the Royalty are at the Palace of Instruction." In Anne's letter of the same date we have the following: "How will it be when we open this paper and the one Emily has written? I wonder whether the Gondaland (*sic*) will still be flourishing, and what will be their condition? I am now engaged in writing the fourth volume of Solala Vernon's life." Next, as Mr. Shorter says: "let us take up the other two little scraps of paper. They are dated July the 30th, 1845, i.e., on Emily's twenty-seventh birthday." There are several entries referring to family matters, but all that is immediately to our purpose is as follows: "Anne left her situation at Thorp Green of her own account, June, 1845. Anne and I went our first long journey by ourselves together, leaving home on the 30th June, Monday, sleeping at York, returning to Keighley Tuesday evening, sleeping there and walking home on Wednesday morning. . . . And during our excursion we were, Ronald Macalgin, Henry Angora, Juliet Augusteena, Rosabella Esmaldan, Ella and Julian Egremont, Catharine Navarre and Cornelia Fitzaphnold, escaping from the Palaces of Instruction to join the Royalists, who are hard driven at present by the victorious Republicans. The Gondals still flourish bright as ever. I am at present writing a work on the First War.* Anne has been writing some articles on this and a book by Henry Sophona. We intend sticking firm by the rascals as long as they delight us, which I am glad to say they do at present."

So much for the letter as far as it reveals Emily's literary occupations at this particular time, July 30th, 1845. But it has a further interest for us, so we will quote another extract: "We are all in decent health only that papa has a complaint in his eyes, and with the exception of B. (Branwell) who, I hope, will be better and do better here-

*Also "The Life of the Emperor Julius," *vide* Anne's letter *infra*.

after. I am quite contented for myself: not so idle as formerly, altogether as hearty, and having learnt to make he most of the present, and not long for the future with the fidgetiness that I cannot do all I wish; seldom or ever troubled with nothing to do, and merely desiring that everybody could be as comfortable as myself, and as undesponding, and then we should have a very tolerable world of it. . . . I must hurry off now to my turning and ironing. I have plenty of work on hand, and writing, and am altogether full of business."

The value of these letters lies in the fact that they are the only pieces of self-revelation Emily Brontë ever vouchsafed to any member of her family. Closely analysed, what do they prove about the writer?

We find her possessed of a spirit of humorous playfulness, a great love of fun and of romantic as contrasted with realistic invention. She is absorbed in the Gondals and their fortunes, and is busy writing about them. We find her also full of a tender affection towards her younger sister, and towards her brother, concerning whom she is quite optimistic. She is, in fact, full of brightness and hope for everyone. We see in her one of the helpers of the world, a lifter of other people's burdens, glorying in her strength. And yet it is this bright and brave creature, hating every species of depression, who is to be credited with the creation of the dark, hopeless, tragic story unfolded in the gloomy pages of "Wuthering Heights."

Next let us take a glance at Anne's letter of the same date. After referring enigmatically to her "escape" from Thorp Green, where, she remarks, "I have had some very unpleasant and undreamt-of experience of human nature," she refers to her brother who has "been a tutor there, and has had much tribulation and ill-health. He was," she goes on, "very ill on Thursday, but he went, with John Brown, to Liverpool, where he is now, I suppose; and we hope he will be better and do better in future. . . . Emily is engaged in writing the Emperor Julius's life. She has read some of it, and I very much want to hear the rest. She is writing some poetry too. I wonder what it is about. I have begun the third volume of 'Passages in the Life of an Individual.' We have not yet finished our Gondal Chronicles that we began three and a half years ago."*

This extract is important, as it refers to what Emily was doing at this time, and confirms her own admission that she was working at Gondal subjects. It will be noticed that there is very little reference to Charlotte throughout the letters. She was evidently not admitted to this confidential gossiping chronicle between the two younger sisters, and probably knew nothing of the Gondal literature. The whole scheme of the Gondal History appears as a "secret" between Anne and Emily, and no one else was allowed to be concerned in its creation.

The "Poems" here referred to, and about which Anne was curious, were a very secret and private possession of Emily's. No one had been permitted to see them, and, but for an accidental

* For these letters in full, see "Brontës and their Circle," p. 134-140.

discovery of them by Charlotte shortly after this letter was written, it is possible they would never have been made known in Emily's lifetime. We know how Charlotte finally persuaded her sister to allow her to publish them, and how for the purpose of anonymity Charlotte suggested they should assume the pseudonyms of the three "Bells." Poetry was indeed Emily's greatest gift. Poetic inspiration was the very breath of her nostrils.

But a close examination of Emily's own work, both at this period, when, as we have seen, she was absorbed with the "Gondals," writing the "History of the First War" and "The Emperor Julius's Life," when most of her poetry was written, must convince any unprejudiced critic that realistic fiction was not at all in her line. Anne and Charlotte were vivid realists: they used all the scanty material that lay to hand, their own schooldays, or their teaching experiences, varied and enriched with a vein of romance or a fiery eruption of passion working through the dull grey lava of composition. Not so Emily. Her mind was outside all these mundane desires and experiences; it was out on the moors, or even above the moors, soaring up to the fantastic companies among whom she had dwelt so long; not degraded to the drunken ravings of a Hindley Earnshaw, or the demoniac machinations of a Heathcliff, or even occupied with the placid, practical-minded prosings of a Mrs. Nelly Dean. Emily's imagination was peopled with beings of another world altogether. She was, like Blake, a visionary of the purest exaltation. Men and women of the usual individual types, that is, as men and women, did not appeal to her; she avoided them on every occasion, indeed fled before them. Charlotte lets this slip inadvertently, in a letter to Mr. Williams: "I should much, very much, like to take that quiet view of the 'Great World' you allude to. . . . Ellis, I imagine, would soon turn aside from the spectacle in disgust. I do not think he admits it as his creed that 'the proper study of mankind is man'—at least not the artificial man of cities."* Not

* "The Brontës and their Circle," p. 148.

indeed man anywhere! One can as soon imagine John Milton writing a novel as Emily Brontë.

One has only to read her inspired poetry to feel how far above earth her spirit waged its warfare: her love was never given to an earthly human lover. Her body was on earth, but her mind and spirit were far above, out and away beyond it. Like "Bonny Kilmeny" she "had been she knew not where," and her "eyes had seen what she could not declare"; she had been, like Kilmeny,

> "Where the cock never crew,
> Where the rain never fell, and the wind never blew,
> But it seemed as the harp of the sky had rung,
> And the airs of Heaven played round her tongue,
> When she spake of the lovely forms she had seen,
> And a land where sin had never been."

She was in fact completely absorbed in her dream-world, the world of the Gondialand. She was not interested enough in them to write about any earthly horses or stables, either at the Heights or at Thrushcross Grange: riding only the winged steeds of her fiery imagination, "the Horse Black Eagle I rode at the Battle of Zamorna." Many of her poems are Gondal poems, though we cannot now trace their connection with the History of the Gondals, as the Chronicles have perished, probably destroyed by Charlotte, because appearing too wildly imaginary for the latter-day world in which she moved and had her being. She thought them rather childish, a little too romantic for "grown-ups" to be occupied with. At any rate, they are gone, and much of Emily has perished with them. So withdrawn was Emily's spirit, so intense her reserve, that even to her darling sister Anne she had not confided a line of her Poems, so that we can but faintly imagine her fury when Charlotte discovered and rifled her hidden nest. "It took hours," says Charlotte, "to reconcile her to the discovery I had made, and days to persuade her that such poems merited publication."

Yet it is this Emily, hiding in a locked desk her secretly written verses from the eyes even of her favourite sister, Anne, and so hotly resenting Charlotte's accidental inspection of them; it is this Emily, jealously guarding the Gondialand secret from the rest of the family; it is this fiercely exclusive, passionately self-contained writer, with a personality shy as the most furtive woodland animal, fleeing from contact with its fellows, shunning and even dreading every kind of publicity—this is the Emily who, we are invited to believe, offered a novel to the public gaze, and asked Charlotte to arrange for its publication. Can we really believe this?

It is true that her poems were finally laid before the public under an assumed name, but we have seen how, much against her will, they were torn from her by Charlotte. Had Charlotte not unearthed them, it is quite certain Emily would never have disclosed their existence. It is surely obvious that at this date, the winter of 1845-6, any idea of writing for the public had never so much as crossed Emily Brontë's mind. She had none of the cravings that devoured her sister Charlotte to make a name in the world. Indeed, Charlotte admits in the "Biographical Notice of her Sisters," prefixed to the 1850 edition of "Wuthering Heights," what difficulty she had to "fan" even the tiny spark of latent ambition in Emily's mind, which makes her calm production of the novel of

"Wuthering Heights" a mysterious and inexplicable thing—unless, that is, we may accept the hypothesis that she was acting on behalf of a concealed author.

But, apart from Emily Brontë's distaste for publicity, there are other considerations and arguments induced by a study of her peculiar personality which make it difficult to imagine her as the author of this book. No work such as "Wuthering Heights" could possibly be produced without some *raison d'être,* and where can we find any *raison d'être* for Emily's authorship? Men and women are not stirred up to write passionate works unless they have experienced something of such passions themselves, and this terrible story is utterly out of harmony with what we know of her spiritual or her visionary nature. It is sharply in contrast with her calm, helpful attitude towards others, that high, brave, contented outlook which made her anxious that everyone should be as cheerful as herself, so that there could be a "very tolerable world" for those around her. The author of "Wuthering Heights" did not find the world tolerable, or care whether it was so or not, or tend to make it more so by his writings. From the ethical point of view the book will not help anyone, masterpiece though it be. It is, on the contrary, one of the most depressing works ever written, and the misery of the chief characters in it is never relieved until the very end. To write such a book would never have suited Emily. She was not out to upset the world: it was hard enough to have to upset Charlotte, who took the hearing of it so badly.

As for the suggestion made both by Sir Wemyss Reid and Miss Robinson, that Emily drew the study of Heathcliff from her unfortunate brother's experiences, that she was so cruelly detached from human sympathy as to "use" his vices for her own artistic ends, and so "drew its profit from her brother's shame," the suggestion is an outrage on this loving guardian of her brother. If we interpret that fiery nature aright, we must believe that Emily would rather have bitten out her tongue or burnt off the offending hand than have uttered or penned a line that should defame him.

There was undoubtedly something in Emily's attitude about the book which puzzled Charlotte, though she could not precisely define it even to herself. She was, as we have seen, shocked beyond measure at its subject matter and language, and nearly all her references to it, both in her letters to Mr. Williams and in her 1850 Preface, are more or less apologetic. Emily, as we have seen, would not discuss the book with her, or answer any questions, even had Charlotte dared to put them. We gather the impression that Charlotte was not a little frightened by her younger sister, of whom she significantly observes in her biographical introduction to the work: "My sister Emily was not a person of demonstrative character, nor one on the recesses of whose mind and feelings even those nearest and dearest to her could, with impunity, intrude unlicensed"; and elsewhere, in a letter to Miss Nussey, we find her complaining that "it is useless to question her—you get no answers."

Yet the fact remains that, when Charlotte appealed to Emily for a novel to offer for publication, Emily produced "Wuthering Heights," and that, after Emily's death, Charlotte, by arrangement with her own publishers, wrote a special Preface to it, claiming the work as Emily's. How then can we account for Charlotte's positive affirmation of her sister's authorship, made in good faith, and duly, if tardily, accepted by the public? If Emily did not write it, then how or why did she "produce" it? For its appearance as coming from Emily Brontë is only less marvellous than Jove's reputed production of Minerva from his brain: on the other hand, if Branwell wrote it, there is no marvel.

It is not incompatible with what we know of Emily Brontë's espousal of all weak and helpless things and causes that she should strain every nerve to rouse and encourage her weak and nerve-wracked brother's ambitions and genius. We have, at any rate, good reason to believe that Emily and Branwell were peculiarly attached to each other, and that her care of him came to absorb a great part of her life. In this we have the support of Miss Mary F. Robinson's account of Emily's devotion, and she probably got it from Miss Nussey; there is also the strong village tradition referred to by Mrs. Chadwick. According to Miss Robinson, it was Emily who waited up for him at night, and let him into the Parsonage long after the other members of the family had retired to bed. After his death, too, according to the old servants, it was Emily who mourned most for her brother. "She died of a broken heart for love of her brother," is the report of Martha Brown's sister.* In the close intimacy obtaining between them at this time, it is inconceivable that Branwell should not have confided to a beloved and loyal sister the project of a novel upon which, we shall show later, he was concentrating his efforts. I think on the evidence we are justified in sketching out what really happened something on these lines. He read it to her as he went along; gave her the parts he had already completed, told her what plot and sequel he had planned. After the first burst of energy in its creation was spent, his volatile nature flagged in the determination to

* Chadwick, "In the Footsteps of the Brontës," p. 361.

complete. Emily urged him to continue, and offered to help him with the copying or with the more tedious parts of composition, and finally pressed him to end it on that note of hopefulness which flashes like evening sunlight through the general gloom in which the story is shrouded.

We may believe, moreover, that Emily was deeply impressed with the work, and pressed her brother to show it, or to let her show it to Charlotte, who was so full of literary projects for the family —Branwell excepted ; and we may equally believe that Branwell, smarting under the sting of Charlotte's reproaches, refused ; that keenly resenting Charlotte's neglect, and the fact of her ignoring his " Poems " when she arranged for the publication of her own and her sisters' efforts, his pride was roused ; that one of the conditions he made with Emily, when he showed her his work, was that it should be kept a secret from the rest of the family, especially from Charlotte. Only Emily should know ; he was certain he could trust her. Had he even wished to let Charlotte see his handiwork, he would never have dared to face her with the subject of that work. The whole terrible story of one man's infatuation for the wife of another, his cold-blooded schemes to get possession of her, his deliberate revenge upon the family of the man and woman who had wronged and thwarted him, if presented by a brother who had just been dismissed in disgrace for a similar unlawful passion, with which Charlotte was completely out of sympathy, would have made the work abhorrent to her; she would have indignantly refused to have anything to do with it. Reading into her brother's character much of Heathcliff's depravity of mind; viewing the work as the outcome of his low or coarse associations; drawing consequently the worst possible conclusions as to the company he frequented; arguing that from these sources alone could he have gleaned the dreadful details and horrible language found in the book: obviously a frank and open appeal to Charlotte was entirely out of the question, and Emily was probably induced to see this.

Yet her great fear was that Branwell should

" PATRICK'S CHAIR."

Branwell's favourite seat in the parlour of the Black Bull Inn, Haworth.

throw up the book. Emily knew it was important, above all things, for him to find an interest in life, something to take him out of himself, and to keep him from brooding. Her interest stimulated him afresh, difficult though it was to keep him up to it. Charlotte's suggestion in the winter of 1845 or early 1846, that each of her sisters and she herself should write a novel and offer them for publication, gave Emily, in a flash, the lead, the opening she was seeking for Branwell. Why not urge him to finish it and leave it to her to get it offered for publication? She, at all events, would have no hesitation in producing it under a pseudonym, the one which Charlotte had already invented for her, and Charlotte should not be allowed to ask any questions. She had herself no novel to offer, but here was this fine story of Branwell's. His need was great, and Emily was not the one to shrink from a likely attempt. She would shoulder the responsibility, if only he would finish it.

Of course, we do not and cannot know what precisely happened: we can only conjecture.

But, where so many conjectures have been already hazarded about the Brontës, it is not very far-fetched to suppose that this generous sister undertook to help him, both by making a fresh copy of what he had done, and by copying out the remainder until he had finished it: she may have written some connecting portions of the work. Having done all this and being determined that, evading Charlotte's boycott, the novel should have its chance, her only course lay in adopting the work, with her brother's full approbation and gratitude, and becoming its patron and foster-mother. At worst it was only a ruse to keep Branwell's authorship from Charlotte, a pious fraud, completely justified by the very exceptional circumstances. There was no thought of "trickery" in the matter. It was a private arrangement between herself and the author, in fact a kind of literary partnership. There was no fraud in helping to get a brother's book published, acting entirely n his interest and with his consent. It was her secret and Branwell's just as the "Gondal" writings were her secret and Anne's. A mystery, if you like, but as we have seen, all the Brontës were inclined to make a mystery of their writings, especially Emily.

Charlotte, indeed, carried this foible farthest in trying to conceal her authorship of "Jane Eyre" from even her bosom friend, Ellen Nussey: "Though twenty books were ascribed to me, I should own none. I scout the idea utterly. Whoever, after I have distinctly rejected the charge, urges it upon me, will do an unkind and ill-bred thing. If, then, any B-an, or G-an, should presume to bore you on the subject, to ask you what 'novel' Miss Brontë has been 'publishing,' you may just say, with that firmness of which you are the perfect mistress when you choose, that you are authorized by Miss Brontë to say that she repels and disowns every accusation of the kind."*

This denial of publication was a much greater departure from the truth than what we ascribe to Emily; but, in Charlotte's case, the excuse was furnished by Mrs. Gaskell that she had pledged

* "Life," p. 245.

her word to her sisters not to reveal it. Had not Emily a better excuse for preserving Branwell's secret?

Furthermore, we must remember that, in dealing with Emily Brontë, we are up against a strong and exceedingly peculiar personality, a personality so strong indeed that she deemed herself accountable to no one for any course or attitude she chose to pursue or assume. Miss Nussey has said of her that "she was in the strictest sense a law unto herself, and a heroine in keeping to her law."* If Emily thought it right to help Branwell in his urgent need of encouragement, and saw no other way but this, she would pursue it; nothing would stop her; for those she loved she would risk anything. No one dared question her, Charlotte least of all, and she herself volunteered nothing. She declined to enter into any correspondence with the publishers, but treated with them through Charlotte or Anne. With that independence of character which shrank from no issue, she was willing to take on her shoulders all

* "The Brontës and their Circle."

the consequences of this daring action. If the book failed to find a publisher, as it might well do from the strange and tragic character of its contents, no harm was done; if, after publication, it attracted no attention, or was roundly abused, or brought little credit to its author—no matter: "Ellis Bell" would bear the blame, and, as we know, "Ellis" did bear it.

The book had no success in Branwell's lifetime; he only lived eight months after its publication, and was then too far gone in consumption and despair to take any interest in its fate; for by that time the once bright flame of his ambition had sunk so low that scarcely even its embers remained—all his desire for fame was now but as dust and ashes within him. Certainly after its publication he had few opportunities of discussing it with his friends, nor perhaps, till after his death, were they aware of its existence. It was many years before it obtained much, if any, circulation in the neighbourhood of Haworth or Halifax. And, but for Emily, "Wuthering Heights" would never have reached the press, would have been cast into the limbo of Branwell's other unfinished efforts.

Charlotte, however, shocked and mystified by the work itself, had no reason to doubt Emily's authorship of the novel she "produced," though she had no direct evidence from Emily herself. As even her stout champion, Miss Sinclair, has to admit: "She left no record, not a note or a word to prove her authorship."

VI

WUTHERING HEIGHTS—By Branwell?

We must now examine the evidences of Branwell's actual known literary power and achievements, and the particular reasons for believing that he was the author of "Wuthering Heights."

It will be necessary to turn back again to the year 1845, and to the close of the month of July, when Branwell, summarily dismissed from his tutorship, had returned home, because it was during the months immediately following his return that his literary activities, already alluded to, have a special significance in connection with our enquiry.

During the time when so many of Branwell's critics suppose that he was giving his entire leisure to drink and dissipation, we have his own evidence, taken from a letter he wrote to his friend Leyland in September, 1845, less than two months after he left Thorp Green, that he had long been turning over a great literary project in his mind. This was the preparation of a novel in three volumes. His own words are as follows:

"I have, since I saw you at Halifax, devoted my hours of time, snatched from downright illness, to the composition of a three-volume novel, one volume of which is completed, and, along with the two forthcoming ones, has been really the result of half a dozen by-past years of thoughts about, and experience in, this crooked path of life. I feel that I must rouse myself to attempt something, while roasting daily and nightly over a slow fire, to while away my torments; and I know that, in the present state of the publishing and reading world, a novel is the most saleable article. . . . My novel is the result of years of thought; and if it gives the vivid picture of human feelings for good and evil, veiled by the cloak of deceit which must enwrap man and woman; if it records as faithfully as the pages that unveil man's heart in 'Hamlet' or 'Lear' the conflicting feelings and clashing pursuits in our uncertain path through life, I shall be as much gratified (and as much astonished) as I should be if, in betting that I could jump the Mersey, I jumped over the Irish Sea. It would not be more pleasant to light on Dublin instead of Birkenhead than to leap from the present bathos of fictitious literature to the firmly fixed rock honoured by the foot of a Smollett or a Fielding.

"That jump I expect to take when I can model a rival to your noble Theseus, who haunted my dreams when I slept after seeing him. But meanwhile I can try my utmost to rouse myself from almost killing cares, and that alone will be its own reward."*

In commenting upon this letter there are several points to notice. First of all, it is evident that for many months before he left Thorp Green, Branwell had been working on a novel, seeing that the first volume of it was completed by September, 1845. This would mean then that the idea of a novel as the most profitable and saleable species of literature had in all probability

* "Leyland," II, p. 83-84.

been suggested by him to Charlotte or Anne in their Christmas or other gathering at the Parsonage, and Charlotte had been quick to take up the idea, and had commenced operations already, privately of course, with the "Professor." Anne also had started on her "Passages in the Life of an Individual," afterwards produced as "Agnes Grey."

Another point is that, as Branwell's novel was one inspired by "half a dozen by-past years of thoughts about and experience in this crooked path of life," it was obviously a recital of some of the things in his own life. But his story was, he tells us, "veiled by the cloak of deceit which must enwrap man and woman," which may be taken to mean that, though he had used his own real experiences and those of some other person, he had covered up these experiences in such a "veiled" wrapping that they would not be easily recognized. That the story was a tragic revelation of the passions of the human heart, morbid, unhappy, despairing and stormy, may be deduced from the comparison with such revelations as those of "Lear" and "Hamlet." The presentation of the picture was "vivid," and it was not written in the current style of "fictitious" literature, but in the simple, realistic style of Smollett or Fielding. All these characteristics of Branwell's novel apply to the tragic story of "Wuthering Heights." It will further be noticed that Branwell refers to the remaining volumes as "forthcoming," an expression that may be taken to imply that, though not, like the first volume, completed, they were actually in hand. Branwell then was working hard at this novel, in the autumn of 1845, to "rouse himself from killing cares" and "while roasting over a slow fire" of mental torment, in which his recent experiences at Thorp Green would be continually present to his mind, and would indubitably colour his narrative. And he was thus steadily and passionately employed on this work, in which he gave free play to his feelings, at the very time when he is represented by his detractors, encouraged by Charlotte's reports, as being entirely given up to the consumption of drink and opium.

We get other glimpses of Branwell's novel, and his tragic subject, from an account given by a friend of his, Mr. William Dearden, who was induced many years later, by a query concerning the authorship of "Wuthering Heights," to communicate to the *Halifax Guardian*, of June, 1867, some "facts within his personal knowledge" relating to the authorship of that work. Having entered on a friendly poetic contest with Branwell, they were to meet at a small hostelry on the road to Keighley, where, under the presidency of Mr. Leyland, each was in turn to read his production. By an annoying mischance Branwell had brought the wrong papers with him, and drew from his hat, where it was convenient to carry notes, the MSS. of a novel he was writing. "Chagrined at the disappointment he had caused," says Mr. Dearden, "he was about to return the papers to his hat, when both friends earnestly pressed him to read them, as they felt a curiosity to see how he could wield the pen of a novelist. After some hesitation he complied with the request, and riveted our attention for about an hour. . . .

The story broke off abruptly in the middle of a sentence, and he gave us the sequel *viva voce,* together with the real names of the prototypes of his characters; but, as some of these personages are still living, I refrain from pointing them out to the public. He said he had not yet fixed upon a title for his production, and was afraid he should never be able to meet with a publisher who would have the hardihood to usher it into the world. The scene of the fragment which Branwell read, and the characters introduced into it—so far as then developed—were the same as those in "Wuthering Heights," which Charlotte Brontë confidently asserts was the production of her sister Emily."*

Now, Branwell's emphatic remark that he feared he would never meet with a publisher who would have the "hardihood" to print his novel indicates that the story was of a terrible nature, one which it would require some courage to publish. Further, from Mr. Dearden's identification of some of the characters, as given him by Branwell, we gather

* "Leyland," II, p. 186-188.

that the scene was laid somewhere in the neighbourhood of Keighley or Halifax. Such indeed was the setting of "Wuthering Heights," on a wild moorland-side, overlooking a valley.

But there is further evidence concerning this novel of Branwell's. Another friend of his, Mr. Edward Sloane, of Halifax, author of some "Essays, Tales and Sketches" (1849), declared to Mr. Dearden that Branwell had read to him, portion by portion, the novel as it was produced at the time, insomuch that he no sooner began the perusal of "Wuthering Heights," when published, than he was able to anticipate the characters and incidents to be disclosed."*

All this seems convincing testimony, and cannot by any species of critical jugglery be got out of the way. Even if Branwell's own statement were to be called in question, it would be ridiculous to suppose that there was a conspiracy on the part of several witnesses at different times and places to assert his authorship. These men were of known position and integrity, Yorkshiremen too, with the

* Quoted "Leyland," II, p. 188.

THE WITHENS, HAWORTH.
Supposed site of "Wuthering Heights."

characteristic Yorkshire straightforwardness of character, and hatred of fabrication. It is impossible they can all have been mistaken, and their statements, added to Mr Grundy's report of Branwell's claim, which his sister verified, form consecutive links in a strong chain of evidence. In ordinary circumstances this evidence would have been considered sufficiently substantial to prove Branwell's case. How then, it may be asked, does it come about that his claim has lain so long in abeyance and not been more urgently pressed?

The reason is not far to seek. The first point is Mrs. Gaskell's impeachment of him, directed, as even Miss Sinclair admits, to account for what seemed, to the prudish mid-Victorian mind, the "coarseness" of "Jane Eyre." To explain Charlotte's apparent aberrations from the path of modesty, it had to be revealed that she had a shocking brother, no wonder her mind dwelt on such ideas, and so forth. Therefore, as Miss Sinclair admirably* points out, "Branwell must be made as iniquitous as it is possible for a young

* Preface to Mrs. Gaskell's "Life of Charlotte Brontë."

man to be." Consequently, when the glory of the book began to dawn on its more discriminating readers, it was felt that such a reprobate as Branwell should not be credited with anything so fine. It was out of the question that such a miserable specimen of humanity as he was continually represented to be could by any possibility have conceived and carried through so great a literary project. Further, Mr. Dearden's challenge in the above-quoted evidence was not available till the 'sixties and 'seventies, when Charlotte was dead; and Charlotte, in her preface to the 1850 edition, had given the stamp of her authority to Emily Brontë's authorship, which was henceforth accepted, though rather grudgingly, by many of the critics, who still averred it could never have been written by a woman, and indeed only by a very exceptional man. To many it resembled the dream of an opium-eater* rather than a tale of human flesh and blood.

But, with Charlotte's preface, the authorship seemed settled. Many who had read it in the

* Sir Wemyss Reid, Lecture on the Brontës.

original edition did not perhaps see this ascription, and, with the interest attached to Emily's Poems, she began to be regarded as something very exceptional from the common rank of authors, capable perhaps of so daring and, on the face of it, so improbable a flight as this. For her "Poems" were beginning to bring her fame. Men like Arnold and Swinburne studied her, and recorded their verdict upon her greatness. The great men of the nineteenth century were chivalrously sympathetic to feminine genius. They remembered Miss Burney, Miss Austen, George Eliot and George Sand, and here now in their midst were these wonderful Brontës. When the protests of the Yorkshire friends of Branwell appeared, they probably never reached the great literary world of London, or, if they did, they passed unheeded, being regarded merely as the personal opinions of local provincials who did not count in the world of letters. In 1883, Miss Mary F. Robinson (Madame Duclaux), published her "Emily Brontë," and other writers have followed her. Sir Wemyss Reid lectured upon the Brontës, and especially upon "Wuthering Heights." With all this great authority behind the ascription of the novel to Emily's pen, how was it possible to put in a claim for Branwell, a man whose reputation had been given away by his own sister's letters, and whose character was regarded by the leading men of the day as beneath contempt.

At length, however, a champion came forward for poor Branwell in the person of Mr. Francis A. Leyland, the brother of Branwell's friend, the sculptor. In his work on "The Brontë Family," published in 1886, he especially took up the study of Branwell, and on the minds of many thoughtful readers must have left the impression that Charlotte's brother had been very unfairly dealt with. But his account is very diffidently given, and his story of Branwell is so mixed up with the history of the sisters that it has failed to carry due conviction. Mr. Shorter, scenting danger to his heroine, attempted no specific answer to Mr. Leyland's theories and evidence, but tried to minimize any possible effect by the indifferent remark: "it is a dull book, readable only by the

Brontë enthusiast." Following his lead, Miss Sinclair adopted the same attitude. With such redoubtable adversaries in the path it is no easy matter to overthrow or even throw doubts upon the popular legend of the authorship of "Wuthering Heights."

The first reason for identifying the book with that novel on which no one disputes that Branwell was actually engaged, is very significant, though indirect. Just at the time when it ought to have been completed, this strange, wild story, "Wuthering Heights"—a story answering so well to the tale Branwell was basing on the experience of human passions as tragic as those of "Lear" or "Hamlet"—suddenly appears from apparently nowhere, sheltered under the ægis of the literary pseudonym of "Ellis Bell." Surely this is more than a remarkable coincidence?

Of Branwell's capacity to write "Wuthering Heights" none of his intimate friends, those at least who were acquainted with his marked abilities, had any doubt whatever. Miss Sinclair dismisses his pretensions with a flippancy deplorable in so accomplished a writer. Mrs. Gaskell acknowledges that he "was a boy of remarkable promise, and, in some ways, of extraordinary precocity of talent." Her remark has already been quoted: "He was very clever, no doubt; perhaps, to begin with, the greatest genius in this rare family."* Mr. Francis A. Leyland, who had met him on one or two occasions, and who heard much of him from his brother and his friends, writes of Branwell's intellectual powers as something quite outstanding. If it be contended that he was so besotted by drink that his natural gifts were squandered, it must be answered that there is no shred of evidence to support this theory. Branwell was, we know, often intemperate, but never, Mr. Leyland insists, habitually so. And when, it may be asked, has occasional inebriety been an obstacle to literary creation? It was assuredly not so with the great Elizabethans, who were notorious for their joyous drinking bouts, nor was it so in the still more dissipated days of the great Augustans, the days of poor Dick Steele,

* "Life," p. 86.

of Sheridan and his boon companions, nor has it proved so in instances well known in our own day. But to return to Branwell: it is incontestable that up to the autumn of 1845, when he was busy with his novel, he was not habitually intemperate. Apart from the breakdown following the announcement of his dismissal from Thorpe Green, he was steadily employed in literary creation. He was, as he declares to Leyland, " trying his utmost."

We have, on the contrary, evidence from his personal friends that he was at this time at the meridian of his powers. But he was by nature diffident and modest, and probably, like more than one genius who has preceded or followed him, he had no idea how exceptional those powers were, both for masterly observation and the recording of passionate emotion. That these powers had a large field for expression in the novel he was writing is evident from the account of it we have read in his letter to Leyland: it was an attempt to express " a vivid picture of human feelings for good and evil," a picture that should be drawn realistically in the great literary school of Smollett or Fielding.

Let us now turn to the internal evidence of the book itself, and examine how far and in what respects it shows signs of distinctively masculine authorship, and of Branwell's authorship in particular. The very character of this terrible tale should convince any thoughtful or closely observant reader that no woman's hand ever penned "Wuthering Heights." Such, indeed, was the universal opinion of the Press when it first appeared, and it may yet return to that opinion. The internal evidence is all against a woman's authorship, for over every page there hangs an unmistakable air of masculinity that cannot be evaded. If the story takes on a feminine aspect at times it is merely because the recital is for the time being put in the mouth of the old housekeeper, Mrs. Dean; and, in respect to the part dealing with the upbringing of the younger Catharine, I willingly concede that Emily Brontë may have helped considerably. But the whole conception of the story is, from start to finish, a man's, particularly so whenever Mr. Lockwood is represented as dealing directly with the story and nowhere is this more evident than in the first two or three chapters. Before examining these pages I would draw the reader's attention to the description of Thrush Cross Grange, as given by young Heathcliff, who had, of course, never seen any place more civilized than the Heights Farm. "Ah! it was beautiful," he exclaims, "a splendid place carpeted with crimson, and crimson-covered chairs and tables, and a pure white ceiling bordered by gold, a shower of glass drops hanging in silver chains from the centre and shimmering with little soft tapers." Now this description is so detailed that it must have been copied from a house visited by the writer. Branwell was well acquainted with such a drawing-room at Thorp Green, and it should also be noticed as a curious coincidence that the names of both these houses begin with the same two letters, so that either of them might be blanked as Th—— Gr——.

Searching closely for minuter traces of masculine authorship, even in the first chapter we come across tiny pieces of evidence pointing to the fact that the writer was not only a man but a scholar. Literally on the very threshold not merely of the story, but of the house itself, we meet with a Latin word which would scarcely be known to anyone not conversant with his Livy or his Virgil: I refer to the word "penetralium." I do not think Emily Brontë knew much Latin, if any. Assuredly she was not an advanced student in the classics, as we know Branwell was. Only a classical scholar would have used the term to signify the interior of the house he was about to enter. Other Latin or classical allusions are: the "indigenæ,"* referring to the surly natives of the country-side, and Catharine Earnshaw's remark that those who attempted to separate her from Heathcliff would "meet the fate of Milo!"† Which "Milo" is here referred to is not clear, but the athlete of Crotona was probably in the author's mind. The allusion would be natural to a student of Ovid or Cicero, and familiar enough to Branwell, though not, I submit, to Emily Brontë, who was not

* "Wuthering Heights," (Cassell) Chap. IV., p. 47.
† *ib.* p. 280.

" learned," so Charlotte tells us. We know from Mr. Grundy how fond Branwell was of introducing Greek, Latin or French words into his correspondence. Some other masculine expressions occur in the first chapters which no gentlewoman of the prim and prudish 'forties would have dreamt of using: the reference to the figures of Loves or Cupids over the doorway as " shameless little boys "; the account of the " ruffianly bitch " who tore Lockwood's " heels and coat-laps "; the term applied by Heathcliff to Isabella Linton— " pitiful, slavish, mean-minded *brach* "; the curious exclamation of Catharine Linton, " Oh! I'm tired—I'm stalled, Hareton! "*

The curses, the brutal language, Heathcliff's outbursts about " painting the house-front with Hindley's blood! "; the reference to " a beast of a servant," Mrs. Dean's remark, " I could not half tell what an infernal house we had ": all these could never have been introduced into a first novel by a quiet, reserved young woman like Emily Brontë. These coarse and wild expressions

* *ib.* p. 280.

were written by a man who had heard many of them used, for they flow naturally from the mouths of his characters.

There are also some touches in the meditations of Mr. Lockwood which particularly suggest Branwell's personal experiences, and which would never occur to a woman-writer; the passage referring to Lockwood's little adventure at the "seaside," where he was "thrown into the company of a most fascinating creature," and, continues the description, "a real goddess in my eyes, as long as she took notice of me. I 'never told my love' vocally; still, if looks have language, the merest idiot might have guessed I was over head and ears, she understood me at last, and looked a return, the sweetest of all imaginable looks. And what did I do? I confess it with shame—shrunk icily into myself like a snail; at every glance retired colder and farther, till finally the poor innocent was led to doubt her own senses, and, overwhelmed with confusion at her supposed mistake, persuaded her mamma to decamp. By this curious turn of disposition I have gained the reputation of deliberate heartlessness; how undeserved, I alone can appreciate."* Now, could this have been written by a woman: more than this, can anyone imagine it to have been written by Emily Brontë? Other passages pointedly suggest Branwell's authorship; the description of the class of yeoman farmer, with many of whom he was undoubtedly acquainted, "with a stubborn countenance, and stalwart limbs set out to advantage in knee-breeches and gaiters. Such an individual seated in his arm-chair, his mug of ale frothing on the round table before him, is to be seen in any circuit of five or six miles among these hills, if you go at the right time after dinner."†

Branwell knew the kind of men well, and had often visited them at the congenial hour, when he was strolling across the moors around Haworth. One feels this touch is direct from his hand. And what more likely than that, on some such visit, he had been overtaken by one of the pitiless snowstorms he here so graphically describes, and had

* "Wuthering Heights," p. 24. † *ib.*, p. 23.

to wade home, like Mr. Lockwood, "sinking up to the neck in snow, a predicament which only those who have experienced it can appreciate."* Who but one familiar with the appliances of a farm would have referred to Hindley Earnshaw, threatening Heathcliff with "an iron weight used for weighing potatoes and hay"?

It is noticeable how the writer dallies—as it were—with the subject of consumption, just as Branwell does in his "Poems to Caroline." This dwelling on the marks of death and decay was a very marked characteristic of Branwell's work, but we can hardly imagine Emily lingering over the description of disease, she who scorned its very existence, and utterly refused to acknowledge herself ill when to the eyes of others she was visibly dying.

One very marked feature of the book is its almost vicious attack upon the canting hypocrisy of the extreme Methodists. The scathing satire on the interminable discourses of these Ranters, and their endless personal exhortations, from

* "Wuthering Heights," p. 46.

which Branwell may often have been the victim, occupies a couple of pages in the third chapter. The subject is raised in Mr. Lockwood's dream, induced by the perusal of Catharine Earnshaw's books, one of which is entitled "A Pious Discourse delivered by the Reverend Jabez Branderham, in the Chapel of Gimmerden Sough."

"In my dream, Jabes had a full and attentive congregation; and he preached—good God! what a sermon: divided into four hundred and ninety parts, each fully equal to an ordinary address from the pulpit, and each discussing a separate sin. Where he searched for them I cannot tell. He had his private manner of interpreting the phrase, and it seemed necessary the brother should sin different sins on every occasion. Oh, how weary I grew. How I writhed and yawned; and nodded and revived! How I pinched and pricked myself, and rubbed my eyes, and stood up, and sat down again, and nudged Joseph to inform me if he would ever have done."* But I need not quote further, the readers will be familiar

* "Wuthering Heights," p. 39.

with the most vivid parody of a Ranter's sermon to be found in our language.

Yet another feature of the work is the grim humour inspiring the writer's satirical sketch of Joseph. An illustration of this occurs almost in the first page, in the comment made by Lockwood upon Joseph's ejaculation, "The Lord help us!" while "looking meantime in my face so sourly that I charitably conjectured he must have need of Divine aid to digest his dinner." Again, another touch is given us in the description of the "immense consolation" Joseph derived from the thought that, although Hareton's soul was destined to perdition, "Heathcliff must answer for it," whereby the ultimate avenging would be at Heathcliff's expense: this saturnine humour is not a woman's, least of all Emily's.

The whole delineation of Joseph is indeed so obviously studied from the life, built up from a model with which the writer was intimately acquainted, created almost with real joy as if to work off some personal grudge against a person of the ranting, Methodist type, from whose pious adjurations the writer had perhaps suffered, that it may be taken as a notable instance of Branwell Brontë's known power of caricature. How well he was able to hit off, in a few lines, certain rough types of character is illustrated for us quite remarkably in a letter he wrote in the beginning of 1840 and to which I have already referred. This letter has been quoted, especially by Miss Robinson, as a sign of Branwell's early depravity, but I propose to quote it here for a quite different purpose. Written by a boy of twenty-one in a roystering vein of merriment, never intended to be seen by any other than his old friend, John Brown, the sexton, to whom it was addressed, it runs as follows:

BROUGHTON-IN-FURNESS,
March 13*th*, 1840.

OLD KNAVE OF TRUMPS,

Don't think I have forgotten you, though I have delayed so long in writing to you. It was my purpose to send you a yarn as soon as I could find materials to spin one with, and it is only just now that I have had time to turn myself round and know where I am. If you saw me now, you would not know me, and you would laugh to hear the character the people give me. Oh, the falsehood and hypocrisy of this world! I am fixed in a little retired town by the sea-shore, among wild woody hills that rise round me—huge, rocky, and capped with clouds. My employer is a retired county magistrate, a large landowner, and of a right hearty and generous disposition. His wife is a quiet, silent, and amiable woman, and his two sons are fine, spirited lads. My landlord is a respectable surgeon, and six days out of seven is as drunk as a lord! His wife is a bustling, chattering, kind-hearted soul; and his daughter!—oh! death and damnation! Well, what am I? That is, what do they think I am? A most calm, sedate, sober, abstemious, patient, mild-hearted, virtuous, gentlemanly philosopher,—the picture of good works, and the treasure-house of religious thought. Cards are shuffled under the table-cloth, glasses are thrust into the cupboard, if I enter the room. I take neither spirits, wine or malt liquors. I dress in black, and smile like a saint or martyr. Everybody says, 'What a good young gentleman is Mr. Postlethwaite's tutor!' This is a fact, as I am a living soul, and right comfortably do I laugh at them. I mean to continue in their good opinion. I took a half-year's farewell of old friend whiskey at Kendal on the night after I left. There was a party of gentlemen at the Royal Hotel, and I joined them. We ordered in supper and whiskey-toddy as 'hot as hell'! They thought I was a physician, and put me in the chair. I gave sundry toasts, that were washed down at the same time, till the room spun round, and the candles danced in our eyes. One of the guests was a respectable old gentleman with powdered hair, rosy cheeks, fat paunch and ringed fingers. He gave 'The Ladies' . . . after which he brayed off with a speech; and in two minutes, in the middle of a sentence, he stopped, wiped his head, looked wildly round, stammered, coughed, stopped again, and called for his slippers. The waiter helped him to bed.

Next a tall Irish squire and a native of the land of Israel began to quarrel about their countries; and, in the warmth of argument, discharged their glasses each at his neighbour's throat instead of his own. I recommended bleeding, purging and blistering; but they administered each other a real 'Jem Warder,' so I flung my tumbler on the floor too, and swore I'd join 'Old Ireland!' A regular rumpus ensued, but we were tamed at last. I found myself in bed next morning, with a bottle of porter, a glass and a corkscrew beside me. Since then I have not tasted anything stronger than milk-and-water, nor, I hope, shall, till I return at midsummer; when we will see about it. I am getting as fat as Prince William at Springhead, and as godly as his friend, Parson Winterbotham. My hand shakes no longer, I ride to the banker's at Ulverston with Mr. Postlethwaite, and sit drinking tea, and talking scandal with old ladies. As to the young ones! I have one sitting by me just now—fair-faced, blue-eyed, dark-haired, sweet eighteen—she little thinks the devil is so near her!

I was delighted to see thy note, old squire, but I do not understand one sentence—you will perhaps know what I mean. . . . How are all about you? I long to see and hear them again. How is 'The Devil's Thumb,' whom men call ———, and the 'Devil in Mourning,' whom they call———. How are ———, and ———, and the Doctor; and him who will be used as the tongs of hell—he whose eyes Satan looks out of, as from windows—I mean ———, esquire? How are little ———, —'Longshanks,' ———, and the rest of them? Are they married, buried, devilled, and damned? When I come I'll give them a good squeeze of the hand; till then, I am too godly for them to think of. That bow-legged devil used to ask me impertinent questions which I answered him in kind. Beelzebub will make of him a walking-stick! Keep to thy teetotalism, old squire, till I return; it will mend thy body. . . . Does 'Little Nosey' think I have forgotten him? No, by Jupiter! nor his clock either. I'll send him a remembrancer some of these days! But I must talk to someone prettier than thee; so goodnight, old boy, and

Believe me thine,

THE PHILOSOPHER.

Write directly. Of course you won't show this letter; and, for Heaven's sake, blot out all the lines scored with red ink."*

This letter, written in the vein of Prince Hal to his jolly old boon-companion Falstaff, is merely a natural outburst of youth and exceeding high spirits, compelled for the sake of earning a stipend to don the decorous garb of the staid young tutor. Branwell, as he says more than once, hated hypocrisy: he disliked having to be other than he naturally was, just as his sisters suffered from having to adopt the irksome work of governessing. He was very young, and felt he must let himself "go" to somebody, hence this letter, as good as anything in Smollett, Dickens or Fielding, an example of wild, rollicking, natural human spirits trying to escape from the toils of propriety and unnatural decorum.

* "Leyland," I., p. 255-9.

It is amazing that readers of this racy and forcible epistle have failed to discover in it a strong vein of that rich but sardonic humour, that headlong torrent of denunciation which pervades the pages of "Wuthering Heights." In his contempt for hypocrisy and irritation at the meddlesome impertinence of some "bow-legged devil" (possibly some local ranting Dissenter, whose sermonizing was particularly distasteful) lies the germ of the subsequent delineation of Joseph, in whose character the author revels with a kind of triumphant maliciousness for which no woman could have had even a faint incentive.

Of the remaining references in the letter we can identify none, but there is one of which we must take special notice, inasmuch as it furnishes decided evidence for Branwell's authorship. The reference I mean is to him "who will be used as the tongs of hell—he whose eyes Satan looks out of, as from windows, I mean ——— esquire?"

It is obvious that even at this date—1840—Branwell Brontë's imagination was playing round some fierce, lowering, gloomy personality with whom he was well acquainted and who was in this letter the object of this damning allusion. Now if we recall his letter to Leyland, already quoted, we remember that the project of this novel was the outcome of observations and reflections made during the previous half-dozen years, which would bring us back to the years 1839–40, when this letter to John Brown was written. The project was but dimly outlined in his mind as yet, but with the passing years the conception began to take shape, until, during his two years' residence at Thorp Green, the hot flame of his passion for another man's wife vitalized and brought it forth in the half-human, half-demon shape we know as Heathcliff, concerning whose eyes the very same simile is used: "that couple of black fiends, so deeply buried who never open their windows boldly, but lurk glinting under them like devil's spies," or elsewhere, where Isabella says: "The clouded windows of hell flashed a moment towards me: the fiend which usually looked out, however, was so dimmed and drowned that I did not fear to hazard another sound of derision." Viewed from this standpoint, the importance of this letter can scarcely be overrated, for it displays not merely the torrential force of Branwell's opinions upon certain hostile personalities, but it reveals the original moulds already prepared in his mind, whence some of the rough casts for the characters in his projected novel were taken.

This view is supported by the opinion of Mr. Leyland, a dispassionate and fair-minded man, writing from a close personal acquaintance with the friends of Branwell Brontë. "Those who have heard fall from the lips of Branwell Brontë—and they are few now—all those weird stories, strange imaginings, and vivid and brilliant disquisitions on the life of the people of the West Riding, will recognize that there was at least no opposition between the tendency of his thoughts and those of the author of 'Wuthering Heights.' As to special points in the story, it may be said that Branwell Brontë had tasted most of the passions, weaknesses and emotions there depicted; had loved in frenzied delusion as Heathcliff loved;

as with Hindley Earnshaw, too, in the pain of loss when his ship struck; the captain abandoned his post; and the crew, instead of trying to save her, rushed into riot and confusion, leaving no hope for their luckless vessel. He had too, indeed, manifested much of the doating folly of the unhappy master of the 'Heights'; and finally, there is no doubt that he possessed, nevertheless, almost as much force of character, determination, and energy as Heathcliff himself."*

Sir Wemyss Reid—quite unwittingly, because he was counsel engaged on the side of Emily—gives evidence which confirms Mr. Leyland's view and my own. The lecturer's contention is that Branwell provided the study for his sister's work, a suggestion which has been shown, I hope, to be an outrage on all we know of Emily Brontë. But his contention that the delineation of Heathcliff's passion for another man's wife found its counterpart in Branwell's experiences is valuable evidence for his authorship of the work. "Whole pages of the story," he says, "are filled with the

* "Leyland, II, p. 192-193.

ravings and ragings of the villain against the man whose life stands between him and the woman he loves. Similar ravings are to be found in all the letters of Branwell Brontë written at this period of his career; and we may be sure that similar ravings were always on his lips, as moody and more than half mad, he wandered about the rooms of the parsonage at Haworth."* This last assertion, totally unsupported by evidence, may be left out of account. It is just the kind of gratuitious suggestion, with no foundation in fact, that is so scandalously and seditiously supplied by the detractors of Branwell Brontë, and which, alas! has obtained credence simply through its audacity.

But, to continue our quotation: "Nay," he goes on to say, "I have found striking verbal coincidences between Branwell's own language and passages in 'Wuthering Heights.' In one of his own letters there are these words in reference to the object of his passion: 'My own life without her will be hell. What can the so-called love of

* Quoted "Leyland," II, p. 193-4.

her wretched, sickly husband be to her compared with mine?' Now," continues Sir Wemyss, "turn to 'Wuthering Heights,' and you will read these words: 'Two words would comprehend my future—death and hell: existence after losing her would be hell. Yet I was a fool to fancy for a moment that she valued Edgar Linton's attachment more than mine. If he loved with all the powers of his puny being, he couldn't love as much in eighty years as I could in a day.'" Sir Wemyss Reid has really proved too much, and his damaging admissions not only give his case away, but greatly strengthen the case for Branwell's authorship from the resemblance between Heathcliff's expression of his passion and Branwell's own experience.

Mr. Clement Shorter has apologized for taking any notice of Branwell at all, adducing the reason that he was obliged to do so in the face of his "preposterous statement that he wrote 'Wuthering Heights.'" But with all the evidence we have of Branwell's own completion of the first volume of a novel which it would require hardihood to publish; of the fact that he was engaged on it just at the time of his great mental struggle with the passion that devastated him; that his sufferings are, even by a hostile critic, admitted to be just such as are depicted in the soul of Heathcliff; that his powers of caricature and delineation of character were great; that he was, at the time when he began his novel, full of literary ambition and at the zenith of his powers which, by all contemporary accounts, were very uncommon: what, it may be asked, was there "preposterous" in such a statement?

Anyone possessed of unprejudiced judgment must see that the book is the work of one who has actually gone through the "hell" which was slowly consuming Heathcliff; of one who, as Branwell Brontë wrote to Leyland, was writing the book to while away his torments. To have produced the work under such conditions would be far from "preposterous"; would, on the contrary, be extremely natural. The truly "preposterous" theory is that Emily Brontë wrote it.

There still remains the problem as to why

Branwell did not come boldly forward as the author of "Wuthering Heights" in his own remaining lifetime. To this it may be answered that, as the evidence already quoted proves, he did so come forward among his most intimate friends, who probably regarded "Ellis Bell" as his *nom de plume*, and never associated it with Emily Brontë. Also we have seen that in the presence of Mr. Grundy, and before his sister Emily, he did claim the greater portion of the novel as his own work. I have already tried to show that his peculiar position with regard to Charlotte was a sufficient barrier to any open declaration of authorship among his own family; and also we have to remember that, since it was written just at the time of Branwell's love story, he would naturally shrink from any open acknowledgment of having portrayed his unhappy infatuation for a woman well known in the county, whose family would have been greatly incensed at any possible identification that might ensue.

Of these obstacles to open acknowledgment the chief was Charlotte's complete estrangement from her brother. Her entire ignorance of any collaboration between Branwell and Emily led her to assert in later years that her brother knew nothing of his sisters' work.

There is a further point in connection with Branwell's concealment of his authorship from the family. We have to remember that for a year and a half, according to Charlotte, the MS. of "Wuthering Heights" went the round of the publishing houses, only to meet with abrupt and ignominious dismissal, and when at last in September, 1847, it was finally accepted by Mr. Newby, another four months elapsed before he issued it. By this time Branwell had lost all interest in the work. His own health was terribly shattered, he was fast sinking into hopeless physical decline; we know from the letter he wrote to Leyland at the close of 1847, or the opening of 1848, that he was at the end of everything, and had long since resigned any literary or other ambition. After the novel was published, it met with little but contumely from the press, and the notices were for the most part so damaging to the author,

In ascribing "Wuthering Heights" to its true author, it may be asked, who would have rejoiced more than this devoted sister that her secret toil and long burden of anxiety was not undertaken in vain? Who would have been more overjoyed than Emily Brontë that this much loved and deeply lamented brother should, even at long last, have come into the fame which is his own?

APPENDIX

A SELECTION FROM THE POEMS OF PATRICK BRANWELL BRONTË.

BLACK COMB.

FAR off, and half revealed, 'mid shade and light,
Black Comb half smiles, half frowns ; his mighty form
Scarce bending into peace, more formed to fight
A thousand years of struggles with a storm
Than bask one hour subdued by sunshine warm
To bright and breezeless rest ; yet even his height
Towers not o'er this world's sympathies ; he smiles—
While many a human heart to pleasure's wiles
Can bear to bend, and still forget to rise—
As though he, huge and heath-clad on our sight,
Again rejoices in his stormy skies.
Man loses vigour in unstable joys.
Thus tempests find Black Comb invincible,
While we are lost, who should know life so well !

—(*circa* 1840).

SONNET I.

ON LANDSEER'S PAINTING.

The Shepherd's Chief Mourner."—A dog keeping watch at twilight over its master's grave.

THE beams of Fame dry up affection's tears;
And those who rise forget from whom they spring;
Wealth's golden glories—pleasure's glittering wing—
All that we follow through our chase of years—
All that our hope seeks—all our caution fears,
Dim or destroy those holy thoughts which cling
Round where the forms we loved lie slumbering;
But, not with thee—our slave—whose joys or cares
We deem so grovelling—power nor pride are thine,
Nor our pursuits, nor ties; yet, o'er this grave,
Where lately crowds the form of mourning gave,
I only hear thy low heart-broken whine—
I only see thee left long hours to pine
For him whom thou—if love had power—would'st save

SONNET II.

ON THE CALLOUSNESS PRODUCED BY CARE.

WHY hold young eyes the fullest fount of tears?
And why do youthful hearts the oftenest sigh,
When fancied friends forsake, or lovers fly,
Or fancied woes and dangers wake their fears?
Ah! he who asks has known but springtide years,
Or Time's rough voice and long since told him why!
Increase of days increases misery;
And misery brings selfishness, which sears
The heart's first feelings: 'mid the battle's roar,
In Death's dread grasp, the soldier's eyes are blind
To comrades dying, and he whose hopes are o'er
Turns coldest from the sufferings of mankind;
A bleeding spirit oft delights in gore:
A tortured heart oft makes a tyrant mind.

SONNET III.

ON PEACEFUL DEATH AND PAINFUL LIFE.

WHY dost thou sorrow for the happy dead?
For, if their life be lost, their toils are o'er,
And woe and want can trouble them no more;
Nor ever slept they in an earthly bed
So sound as now they sleep, while dreamless laid
In the dark chambers of the unknown shore,
Where Night and Silence guard each sealed door.
So, turn from such as these thy drooping head,
And mourn the dead alive, whose spirit flies,
Whose life departs, before his death has come;
Who knows no heaven beneath Life's gloomy skies,
Who sees no Hope to brighten up that gloom—
'Tis He who feels the worm that never dies—
The real death and darkness of the tomb.

NOTE.—These three Sonnets were, according to Mr. Leyland, written in the year 1842. It will be remembered that in the autumn of this year Branwell attended the deathbed not only of his aunt, Miss Branwell, but of his friend, the Rev. W. Weightman.

THE EPICUREAN'S SONG.

(1842)

THE visits of Sorrow
Say, why should we mourn ?
Since the sun of to-morrow
May shine on its urn ;
And all that we think such pain
Will have departed—then
Bear for a moment what cannot return.

For past time has taken
Each hour that it gave,
And they never awaken
From yesterday's grave ;
So surely we may defy
Shadows, like memory,
Feeble and fleeting as midsummer wave.

From the depths where they're falling
Nor pleasure, nor pain,
Despite our recalling,
Can reach us again ;
Though we brood over them,
Naught can recover them,
Where they are laid they must ever remain.

So seize we the present,
And gather its flowers,
For—mournful or pleasant—
'Tis all that is ours;
While daylight we're wasting,
The evening is hasting,
And night follows fast on vanishing hours.

Yes—and we, when night comes,
Whatever betide,
Must die as our fate dooms,
And sleep by their side;
For change is the only thing
Always continuing;
And it sweeps creation away with its tide.

REAL REST.

(1845-6)

I SEE a corpse upon the waters lie,
With eyes turned, swelled and sightless, to the sky,
And arms outstretched to move, as wave on wave
Upbears it in its boundless billowy grave.
Not time, but ocean, thins its flowing hair;
Decay, not sorrow, lays its forehead bare;
Its members move, but not in thankless toil,
For seas are milder than this world's turmoil;
Corruption robs its lips and cheeks of red,
But wounded vanity grieves not the dead;
And, though these members hasten to decay,
No pang of suffering takes their strength away.
With untormented eye, and heart and brain,
Through calm and storm it floats across the main;
Though love and joy have perished long ago,
Its bosom suffers not one pang of woe;
Though weeds and worms its cherished beauty hide,
It feels not wounded vanity nor pride;
Though journeying towards some far-off shore,
It needs no care nor gold to float it o'er;
Though launched in voyage for eternity,
It need not think upon what is to be;
Though naked, helpless, and companionless
It feels not poverty, nor knows distress.

Ah, corpse! if thou could'st tell my aching mind
What scenes of sorrow thou hast left behind,
How sad the life which, breathing, thou hast led,
How free from strife thy sojourn with the dead;
I would assume thy place—would long to be
A world-wide wanderer o'er the waves with thee!
I have a misery, where thou hast none;
My heart beats, bursting, whilst thine lies like stone;
My veins throb wild, whilst thine are dead and dry;
And woes, not waters, dim my restless eye;
Thou longest not with one well loved to be,
And absence does not break a chain with thee;
No sudden agonies dart through thy breast;
Thou hast what all men covet—REAL REST.
I have an outward frame, unlike to thine,
Warm with young life—not cold in death's decline
An eye that sees the sunny light of Heaven—
A heart by pleasure thrilled, by anguish riven—
But, in exchange for thy untroubled calm,
Thy gift of cold oblivion's healing balm,
I'd give my youth, my health, my life to come,
And share thy slumbers in thy ocean tomb.

SONNET (April, 1846).

When all our cheerful hours seem gone for ever,
All lost that caused the body or the mind
To nourish love or friendship for our kind,
And Charon's boat, prepared, o'er Lethe's river
Our souls to waft, and all our thoughts to sever
From what was once life's Light; still there may be
Some well-loved bosom to whose pillow we
Could heartily our utter self deliver;
And if, toward her grave—Death's dreary road—
Our Darling's feet should tread, each step by her
Would draw our own steps to the same abode,
And make a festival of sepulture;
For what gave joy, and joy to us had owed,
Should Death affright us from, when he would her restore?

Note.—The sentiment expressed in the last four lines of this poem are markedly and strangely suggestive of the feelings of Heathcliff in connection with the entombment of Catherine Linton.